# CHILDREN OF ALCOHOLICS

GARLAND REFERENCE LIBRARY
OF SOCIAL SCIENCE
(VOL. 461)

# CHILDREN OF ALCOHOLICS
## *A Sourcebook*

Penny Booth Page

GARLAND PUBLISHING, INC. • NEW YORK & LONDON
1991

**Library of Congress Cataloging-in-Publication Data**

Page, Penny Booth, 1949–
    Children of alcoholics : a sourcebook / Penny Booth Page.
        p.  cm. — (Garland reference library of social science ; vol.
461)
    Includes index.
    ISBN 0–8240–3045–1
    1. Children of alcoholics—Bibliography. 2. Adult children of
alcoholics—Bibliography. I. Title. II. Series: Garland reference
library of social science ; v. 461
Z7721.P334  1991
[HV5132]
016.36229'23—dc20                                        91–19611
                                                              CIP

Printed on acid-free, 250-year-life paper
Manufactured in the United States of America

For my grandmother, "T" Pennington, who has been an example of love, dignity, and joy of living.

# CONTENTS

# Indexes

# PREFACE

The literature on children of alcoholics is a relatively recent phenomenon. Margaret Cork's book **The Forgotten Children**, published in 1969, was one of the first major studies to examine the emotional and psychological needs of children of alcoholics. Up to that time, the literature on alcoholism had focused primarily on the alcoholic or the disease of alcoholism, with occasional material on the effects of alcoholism on the spouse or the family as a whole. Only a few research studies had looked at such factors as social adjustment and health problems specifically among children of alcoholics (Nylander 1960).

By the early 1980s, however, a children of alcoholics movement had emerged, fueled by popular and professional interest, a growing body of literature, and a network of self-help groups and local and national organizations. This movement has been largely self-generated from the grass-roots level with relatively little guidance from mental health professionals (Steinglass 1989). As the movement has grown, it has, in turn, generated a number of questions that have not been adequately answered by research to date (Johnson and Bennett 1989). This bibliography incorporates the popular, professional, and research literature on this fast-growing topic of interest.

ix

Although such terms as "children of alcoholics," "adult children," and "codependent" appear in most of this literature, their meanings may vary. For many authors (including myself) "children of alcoholics" can refer to any children, regardless of age, with an alcoholic parent, while other authors restrict this term to minor children. "Adult child" is frequently broadened to mean someone who grew up in an alcoholic family or in any family that suffered some major disruption. "Codependent" is a more recent term that may have had its origins in "coalcoholic," a term frequently applied to the enabling behavior of the spouse (Martin 1988). Now, however, it has evolved into a descriptive label that may be applied to anyone whose life has been affected by someone else's addiction or compulsive behavior. Codependents, children of alcoholics, and adult children are often described as coming from "dysfunctional" families--i.e., families that revolve around a problem such as alcoholism, other drug abuse, physical or sexual abuse, or neglect. In this text the abbreviations COA (children of alcoholics) and ACOA (adult children of alcoholics) will be used to avoid over-repetition of these terms.

Most of the literature on children of alcoholics has been published since 1970. A large portion of this material has been anecdotal, reflecting personal experiences of children of alcoholics or the experiences of clinicians working with this population. In addition to the alcohol and drug publishers, such as Hazelden and Health Communications, who specialize in materials on recovery and family issues, several of the major publishing houses, including Harper and Row and Prentice-Hall, have added a substantial number of titles on children of alcoholics or alcohol-related family issues. **Adult Children of Alcoholics** by Janet Woititz (1983) and **Codependent No More** by Melody Beattie (1987) have each sold more than one million copies (Kaminer 1990). Such materials are in popular demand in bookstores and libraries around the country.

## Scope and Arrangement of the Bibliography

This bibliography is intended to serve as a resource for those who are seeking information on children of alcoholics. It describes literature written for and about young children and adult children of alcoholics as well as materials for professionals--counselors, treatment personnel, educators, health professionals, and social service workers--who may deal with COAs among their clients or students. Empirical research studies on the characteristics, problems, and treatment of COAs are also included. Although most items focus specifically on children of alcoholics, some materials on broader family issues are included if they contain separate sections or substantial information about COAs.

The materials covered in this bibliography include books, pamphlets, and journal articles published in English from 1969 to early 1990. Because the number of journal articles is much greater than the number of monographs on this topic, only the more recent journal articles (from 1985 to the present) have been included, with a few exceptions for earlier notable pieces. Each entry provides complete author, title, and publication information as well as a summary of the content. Although no evaluative rating is used, any special strengths or weaknesses are noted in the summaries. Prices for monographs were not included because they change rapidly. There is a publisher's index to help the reader obtain current price and ordering information on any publication.

Certain types of materials were not included in the bibliography. Books of poetry and daily affirmations were excluded since these tend to be more inspirational than informational. Materials dealing primarily with fetal alcohol syndrome (FAS) were also excluded. The literature on FAS is well covered by several excellent bibliographies (Abel 1981 and 1990; Center of Alcohol Studies 1983), which I do not need to duplicate. Some of the materials in this bibliography do include some information on FAS, and these can be located by using the subject index. No posters, games, or audiovisual materials were included unless they were part of a set that also contained written materials (several curricula fall into this multi-media category). Books that describe games or similar exercises as therapeutic tools were included in the treatment chapters; actual board games themselves, however, were not covered.

The number of films, videocassettes, and audiotapes dealing with children of alcoholics and family alcohol issues has grown rapidly in the last decade. To adequately cover this material would require another bibliography. Audiovisual materials are particularly useful with groups such as adolescents or counselors-in-training. A list of producers, distributors, and reviewing sources is provided in Appendix B to aid readers in locating appropriate audiovisual material.

The bibliography is arranged in two parts. Part one covers literature on minor children of alcoholics and also includes items that cover both minor children and adult children. Part two includes literature that focuses primarily on adult children of alcoholics. Each part is divided into chapters covering general reference, research, family issues, treatment, recovery, and fiction. Within the chapters entries are arranged alphabetically by author or title in two sections--books/pamphlets and journal articles. Each chapter begins with a brief scope note describing the types of materials to be found; cross-references are provided at the ends of the chapters to direct the reader to related items elsewhere in the bibliography.

To locate material in the bibliography, the reader can browse through the appropriate chapters or use the indexes to identify specific items. The numbers in the author, title, and subject indexes refer to item numbers rather than page numbers. All publishers cited in the entries are listed alphabetically in the publishers' index with current addresses.

There are three appendixes with additional resource information. Appendix A lists and briefly describes organizations and associations that can provide further information or assistance to children of alcoholics. Appendix B covers the audiovisual resources (described above), and Appendix C provides a brief list of periodicals that regularly or frequently contain material on COAs. All of these resources include current addresses, as well as phone numbers for the organizations and associations.

This is not a comprehensive bibliography. Although I have tried to identify and include as much material as I could on this topic, I cannot claim total success. In addition to those exclusions I have already described, I did not include any material that I was not able to examine personally or for which I could not obtain sufficient information. Any errors or notable omissions in the text are my own. I have tried to provide the reader with a good idea of the quantity, quality, and variety of published information that is currently available on children of alcoholics.

## References

Abel, Ernest L., ed. **Fetal Alcohol Syndrome.** 3 vols. Boca Raton, FL: CRC Press, 1981.

Abel, Ernest L., ed. **New Literature on Fetal Alcohol Exposure and Effects: A Bibliography, 1983–1988.** Westport, CT: Greenwood Press, 1990.

Beattie, Melody. **Codependent No More: How to Stop Controlling Others and Start Caring for Yourself.** Center City, MN: Hazelden, 1987.

Center of Alcohol Studies. **The Fetus and Alcohol.** Alcohol Bibliography Series, B435. New Brunswick, NJ: Rutgers Center of Alcohol Studies, 1983--.

Cork,    Margaret.    The    Forgotten    Children.    Toronto:
    PaperJacks, 1969.

Johnson,   Jeannette   L.,   and   Linda   A.   Bennett.   **Adult
    Children of Alcoholics: Theory and Research.** New
    Brunswick, NJ: Rutgers Center of Alcohol Studies,
    1989.

Kaminer, Wendy. "Chances Are You're Codependent Too."
    *New York Times Book Review* (Feb. 11, 1990): 1, 26-
    27.

Martin, Denise. "A Review of the Popular Literature on Co-
    Dependency." *Contemporary Drug Problems* 15(1988):
    383-98.

Nylander,   I.   "Children   of   Alcoholic   Fathers."   *Acta
    Paediatrica* 49(1960): 9-127.

Steinglass, Peter. "Foreword." In **Group Psychotherapy with
    Adult Children of Alcoholics: Treatment Tools and
    Countertransference** Considerations,   by   Marsha
    Vannicelli, ix-xii. New York: Guilford Press, 1989.

Woititz, Janet G. **Adult Children of Alcoholics.** Deerfield
    Beach, FL: Health Communications, 1983.

## Acknowledgments

I would like to thank several people, without whose help this volume might never have been started--or completed. Sylvia Falk, Janet Pichette, and Cathy Weglarz of the Center of Alcohol Studies library, Rutgers University, helped me to identify resources and shouldered many of my professional duties so that I could devote more time to this project. I am also indebted to Valerie Mead of the New Jersey Alcohol/Drug Resource Center and Clearinghouse for sharing her special expertise in the preparation of the appendix on audiovisual resources. Most of all I want to thank my husband, Mark Lender, for his love, patience, and editorial criticism.

# PART ONE

# CHILDREN OF ALCOHOLICS

# INTRODUCTION

According to the Children of Alcoholics Foundation, there are approximately 28.6 million children of alcoholics in the United States (or one of every eight Americans); of this total, 6.6 million are under the age of eighteen (Russell, Henderson, and Blume 1985). Research and clinical studies have indicated that children of alcoholics are at increased risk for behavioral, emotional, and psychological problems as well as substance abuse, child abuse, and neglect. O'Gorman and Ross (1986) found that 55% of patients at a New York State residential treatment facility for adjudicated male minors came from homes with an alcoholic parent or other adult; 60% of the patients had records of alcohol or other drug problems of their own. In an earlier review of the literature on alcohol and family violence, Spieker (1978) found that 50% of alcoholic parents were child abusers. According to Black's research (1981), 66% of children in alcoholic homes have been physically abused and 26% have been incest victims.

Many of these research studies have been limited by methodological problems such as biased sample groups (e.g., juvenile offenders or children already in treatment), lack of matched control groups for comparison, and failure to consider other environmental or behavioral factors (Johnson and Bennett 1988). While some researchers have looked at risk factors for COAs, other investigators have examined protective factors that have contributed to the successful adjustment of many children of alcoholics.

The professional literature on children of alcoholics includes materials written for counselors, teachers, health professionals, and other social service workers who regularly come in contact with COAs. Much of this material is intended to provide awareness of alcoholism as a family disease in addition to specific information about the needs and problems of COAs. For many years this literature was colored by two misconceptions: that parental abstinence would be sufficient to reverse a family's problems, and that children could not be helped while a parent was still drinking. Research and clinical findings have shown that neither assumption is correct (Macdonald and Blume 1986). The literature covered in this section reflects a wide range of research topics and professional information as well as items written to help COAs understand and cope more effectively within an alcoholic family situation.

## References

Black, Claudia. **It Will Never Happen to Me!** Denver: MAC Publishing, 1982, 136-41.

Johnson, Jeannette L., and Linda A. Bennett. **School-Aged Children of Alcoholics: Theory and Research.** New Brunswick, NJ: Rutgers Center of Alcohol Studies, 1988.

Macdonald, Donald I., and Sheila B. Blume. "Children of Alcoholics." *American Journal of Diseases of Children* 140(1986): 750-54.

O'Gorman, Patricia, and Robert A. Ross. "Children of Alcoholics in the Juvenile Justice Systems." In **Growing in the Shadow: Children of Alcoholics,** ed.

by Robert J. Ackerman, 143-46. Deerfield Beach, FL: Health Communications, 1986.

Russell, Marcia, Cynthia Henderson, and Sheila B. Blume. **Children of Alcoholics: A Review of the Literature.** New York: Children of Alcoholics Foundation, 1985, 1-2.

Spieker, Gisela. "Family Violence and Alcohol Abuse." In **Papers Presented at the Twenty-Fourth International Institute on the Prevention and Treatment of Alcoholism, Zurich 1978,** 335-340. Lausanne, Switzerland: International Council on Alcohol and Addictions, 1978.

# 1. GENERAL REFERENCE

## Books and Pamphlets

The materials in this section include bibliographies, directories, and other general reference tools on children of alcoholics. These references also cover adult children. The items cited in these tools will lead COAs to further sources of help or information on the effects of family alcoholism.

1.     Ackerman, Robert J. **Children of Alcoholics: A Bibliography and Resource Guide.** 3d ed. Deerfield Beach, FL: Health Communications, 1987. 82 pp.

Intended as a resource list of materials and organizations to help professionals working with children of alcoholics. May also be useful to teenage or adult children who want to know where to get further information on alcoholism and its effects on the family. The text is divided into eight categories based primarily on format of material: books, research and articles (including book chapters, conference papers, journal articles, and theses), pamphlets and booklets, films, videocassettes, audiocassettes, miscellaneous (games, slides, newsletters), and agencies. The arrangement of entries varies between sections. Books and articles are listed alphabetically by author, and most items were published between the early 1970s and the mid 1980s. Pamphlets are arranged by

source (publisher or distributor) and then by title; authors
are not always listed. All audiovisuals are listed
alphabetically by title, and most include a brief description
of content as well as length and distributor. Except for the
audiovisual and miscellaneous materials, no other sections
are annotated. Some addresses for publishers and agencies
are outdated. There are no author, title, or subject
indexes.

2.      Barnes, Grace M., and Diane K. Augustino. **Alcohol
        and the Family: A Comprehensive Bibliography.**
        Bibliographies and Indexes in Sociology, no. 9.
        Westport, CT: Greenwood Press, 1987. 461 pp.

        Lists over 6,000 pieces of literature dealing with
issues related to alcohol use within families. Topics covered
range from genetic transmission of alcoholism to family
violence and family therapy and treatment of alcoholism.
Includes journal articles, books, pamphlets, dissertations,
and government reports and fact sheets in English as well
as foreign languages (with original and translated titles).
Although most entries are best suited to a research or
professional audience (e.g., social workers or alcoholism
treatment personnel), there are a number of titles, such as
the Al-Anon publications, appropriate for a lay audience.
This bibliography is exhaustive in its coverage of the
literature from 1900 to the present with most entries from
the last two decades, reflecting the more recent growth of
attention to family alcohol problems. Items are arranged
alphabetically by author and do not contain abstracts;
however, there is a lengthy subject index.

3.      **Children of** Alcoholics. Alcohol Bibliography Series,
        no. B020. New Brunswick, NJ: Rutgers Center of
        Alcohol Studies, 1983--. approx. 60 pp.

        Lists over 600 citations to research and professional
literature on children and adult children of alcoholics.
Materials cited are from the library collections of the

Rutgers Center of Alcohol Studies; they include books, journal articles, dissertations, conference papers, separately-authored book chapters, and government documents. The bibliography is updated annually, and entries are arranged alphabetically by author or title within each updated section. There are no abstracts. This publication is part of a series of bibliographies covering over 100 alcohol topics, including family aspects of alcohol use and treatment of the family.

4.     **Directory of National Resources for Children of Alcoholics.** New York: Children of Alcoholics Foundation, 1986. 158 pp.

Describes over 250 programs throughout the United States and Virgin Islands that provide services specifically designed for children of alcoholics. Programs are arranged alphabetically by state and city within three sections. Section I gives information on programs that provide direct services, such as counseling, prevention, education, or aftercare, to children of alcoholics. Each entry contains address, clientele served, admission criteria, fees and financial assistance, and a listing of program services. Separate information is provided for agencies that have different programs for young children and adult children of alcoholics. Section II describes programs that serve a restricted population, such as programs limited to students within a particular school district. Section III provides abbreviated descriptions of programs that offer indirect services to COAs through public awareness activities, program or curriculum development, and training of counselors, educators, or other professionals who deal with COAs. Alcohol and drug libraries, publishers, and research centers that produce or disseminate information on COAs are not included nor are service programs that treat COAs only as part of a larger population. This is a unique and easy-to-use resource, despite the lack of indexes by program name or type of service.

5.      National Association for Children of Alcoholics.
        **NACoA Resource Guide: Providers of Services for
        Children of Alcoholics and Other Addictions.** South
        Laguna, CA: NACoA, n.d. 72 pp.

        Consists entirely of advertisements for programs or
individuals offering some type of service for children or
adult children of alcoholics. Advertisements range from
full-page ads to copies of business cards and cover a
variety of services including treatment programs,
counseling, professional training, program design and
implementation, and production or distribution of print or
audiovisual materials. There is a very brief introduction to
NACoA that outlines the association goals as well as some
brief facts about COAs. Resources are listed either under a
national heading or under state headings and are entered in
order of receipt by the publisher. The table of contents
serves as an alphabetical index by national and state
categories. Some business cards provide only a name and
phone number with no elaboration as to the services
offered. There is no indication that any professional
criteria must be met to be eligible for listing; professionals
are asked to evaluate the services for themselves before
making referrals. This is one of a very few listings of
resources for COAs.

6.      Windle, Michael. **Children of Alcoholics: A
        Comprehensive Bibliography.** Buffalo, NY: Research
        Institute on Alcoholism, 1989. 105 pp.

        Provides a listing of research studies (books,
chapters, and journal articles) on children and adult
children of alcoholics. The entries are arranged in six topic
areas: biochemical, neuropsychological and
neurophysiological, behavior genetic, temperament and
personality, family, prevention and intervention, and
general (miscellaneous). Each section begins with a
discussion of the type of literature covered; entries are
then arranged alphabetically by author. There are no

annotations. Citations are primarily dated from the 1970s to the late 1980s and were identified from searches of major online databases and published bibliographies covering literature on alcohol and the family.

See also: 19.

## 2. RESEARCH

### Books and Pamphlets

This chapter cites research studies and overviews of research issues related to children of alcoholics. These studies cover biological, genetic, and environmental factors associated with alcoholism in the family, along with studies of treatment approaches and needs of COAs. Items relating to both adult children and younger children are included. Studies focusing only on fetal alcohol syndrome and maternal drinking are excluded.

7.    Booz Allen and Hamilton, Inc. **An Assessment of the Needs and Resources for Children of Alcoholic Parents.** Springfield, VA: National Technical Information Service, 1974. 162 pp.

Prepared from results of a survey conducted for the National Institute on Alcohol Abuse and Alcoholism. This is one of the earliest systematic studies on the needs and services for children of alcoholics. Presents estimates on the number of COAs and identifies common characteristics, problems, and coping mechanisms. Examines the resources available at the time to meet these needs and makes recommendations for their improvement. Although this study is over fifteen years old, it has provided a foundation for the development of more effective services for COAs, and it serves as a yardstick for measuring how far local and national resources have come in serving the needs of this population. References, bibliography.

8.      **Children of Alcoholics.** New York: Haworth Press, 1987. 128 pp.

Contains articles by noted researchers and clinicians on issues related to children of alcoholics. Topics cover policy issues, treatment of adult children, research in genetics and familial transmission of alcoholism, and the influence of socioeconomic factors on occurrence of fetal alcohol syndrome. The final article is a bibliography of resources related to topics discussed in the text. It includes indexing and abstracting sources, current awareness publications, books, journals, handbooks and directories, meetings and proceedings, audiovisuals, and guides to special research centers and library collections. Unfortunately, several major alcohol databases and reference sources are omitted. Also published as *Advances in Alcohol and Substance Abuse*, volume 6, number 4, 1987. References, bibliography.

9.      Cork, R. Margaret. **The Forgotten Children.** Markham, Ontario: PaperJacks Ltd., 1969. 112 pp.

Landmark text based on a study of 115 children of alcoholics aged 10-16. Begins with excerpts from interviews offering the children's perceptions of their family situations. The bulk of the text presents the author's conclusions, based on the interviews, about the feelings, behavior, and development of COAs. Also includes recommendations for more and better treatment services for COAs and nonalcoholic spouses. An appendix describes the methodology of the study. One of the first research studies to address the characteristics and needs of COAs. Still useful for policymakers, as well as prevention and treatment personnel. References.

10.     Goodwin, Donald W. **Is Alcoholism Hereditary?** 2d
        ed. New York: Ballantine Books, 1988. 259 pp.

        Discusses current knowledge and opinion regarding
the influence of genetics and of environment on the
development of alcoholism. Reviews some of the major
research, including twin and adoption studies, that
demonstrate the relative effects of heredity and family
surroundings on an individual's susceptability to alcoholism.
Also provides basic information for the layman on alcohol
and its effects on the body and behavior as well as a
discussion of alcoholism and its related problems. The
author presents an overview of several treatment
approaches--psychotherapy, Alcoholics Anonymous, behavior
therapy, and drug therapy--along with his own
recommendations for the use of antabuse in addition to
counseling. Includes a section on the current children of
alcoholics movement, arguing that research has not proven
sufficient links between COAs and other emotional or
behavioral problems. Notes, references, index.

11.     Griswold-Ezekoye, Stephanie, Karol L. Kumpfer, and
        William J. Bukoski, eds. **Childhood and Chemical
        Abuse: Prevention and Intervention.** New York:
        Haworth Press, 1985. 299 pp.

        Focuses on issues related to the development and
prevention of alcohol and other drug problems among young
children and adolescents. Part I identifies the factors most
commonly associated with youthful alcohol and drug use.
Included is a separate section that reviews the research
literature on family environmental and genetic influences.
The discussion covers biological markers as well as family
behaviors--specifically parental alcohol or drug abuse--that
are highly correlated with childhood substance abuse. Part
II deals with school, community, and family-based programs
for preventing substance abuse by youth, while part III
focuses on the need for intervention and treatment with
this population (including a description of a multicultural
model for prevention and treatment). The prevention and

intervention sections do not cover programs geared specifically for children of alcoholics; however, brief discussions of such programs are provided in the section on family influences. Also published as *Journal of Children in Contemporary Society*, volume 18, number 1-2, 1985. References, indexes.

12.      Johnson, Jeannette L., and Linda A. Bennett. **School-Aged Children of Alcoholics: Theory and Research.** New Brunswick, NJ: Rutgers Center of Alcohol Studies, 1988. 23 pp.

     Summarizes existing research on the effects of parental alcoholism on children aged 5-18. Covers such topics as risk factors versus protective factors for alcoholism and developmental issues related to COAs. Outlines four major research areas on COAs--emotional problems, behavioral adjustment, electrophysiology, and cognition--and briefly describes the findings of important studies in each category. Presents an excellent overview on the current state of scientific and scholarly knowledge regarding COAs; also calls attention to aspects that need further research. Bibliography.

13.      Lewis, David C., and Carol N. Williams, eds. **Providing Care for Children of Alcoholics: Clinical and Research Perspectives.** Deerfield Beach, FL: Health Communications, 1986. 112 pp.

     Presents a critical overview of major research findings, theoretical literature, and policy issues related to the needs of children of alcoholics. Contributors are well-known researchers, physicians, and policy analysts in the alcohol field. The topics cover a wide range of areas including social and cultural factors in alcoholic families, fetal alcohol syndrome, clinical intervention with children of alcoholics, and public policy. References.

14.   National Institute on Alcohol Abuse and Alcoholism.
      **Biological/Genetic Factors in Alcoholism.** NIAAA
      Research Monograph, no. 9., edited by Victor M.
      Hesselbrock, Edward G. Shashan, and Roger E.
      Meyer. Washington, DC: U.S. Government Printing
      Office, 1983. 166 pp.

Reports the proceedings of a workshop to review
biological and genetic factors related to the etiology of
alcoholism. Papers focus primarily on two variables
identified as possible biological risk factors associated with
the development of alcoholism: monoamine oxidase (MAO)
and acetaldehyde (AcH). The possible genetic links to MAO
activity and levels of AcH are examined along with the
effects of environmental factors on these variables. The
implications of these findings for future research and the
development of theoretical models are also discussed.
References, charts, graphs.

15.   National Institute on Drug Abuse. **Youth at High
      Risk for Substance Abuse.** Washington, DC: U.S.
      Government Printing Office, 1987. 181 pp.

Presents the papers and panel discussions from a
technical review meeting on "Special Youth Populations--
What Etiology Suggests About Prevention and Treatment
Programming," sponsored by the National Institute on Drug
Abuse. The review meeting focused on four youth
populations that were seen as high risk for developing
alcohol or other drug problems: children of substance
abusers, juvenile delinquents, children in foster care
programs, and runaways. The section on children of
substance abusers provides a review of research studies on
numbers of children living in substance abusing families
(COSAs), prevalence of problems among COSAs, risk factors
for developing substance abuse (genetic factors, other
biological vulnerabilities, environmental factors), and
psychosocial factors in early childhood development. There
is also a discussion of possible interventions for biomedical
and psychosocial risk factors. References.

16.    Orford, Jim, and Judith Harwin. **Alcohol and the Family.** New York: St. Martin's Press, 1982. 295 pp.

Includes contributions from British and American experts on the effects of alcohol abuse and alcoholism on family members. Chapters provide critical reviews of research and theory on factors associated with family alcohol problems, the role of alcohol in family systems, and provision of treatment services to families of alcoholics. Several chapters focus on topics related to children of alcoholics, including transmission of alcohol problems in the family (hereditary and environmental influences), the impact of alcoholism on children (family and social relationships), and the prevention of alcohol problems in the family. Useful for family therapists or those involved in treatment research. References, index.

17.    **Report of the Conference on Research Needs and Opportunities for Children of Alcoholics.** New York: Children of Alcoholics Foundation, 1984. 23 pp.

Summarizes the discussions and conclusions of a conference in 1984 sponsored by the Children of Alcoholics Foundation. The goal of the conference was to bring together alcohol researchers and experts to discuss the current state of knowledge and to identify future research needs regarding children of alcoholics. Topics include genetic factors in alcoholism, family studies, prevention and treatment, and ethics and public policy issues. The report contains some helpful statistics on the number of children affected by parental alcoholism and the associated problems. References.

18.    Russell, Marcia, Cynthia Henderson, and Sheila B. Blume. **Children of Alcoholics: A Review of the Literature.** New York: Children of Alcoholics Foundation, 1985. 69 pp.

Prepared as a resource document for participants in the 1984 Conference on Research Needs and Opportunities for Children of Alcoholics (see item 17). Contains summaries of research studies on a wide range of COA issues including genetic factors in alcoholism and sensitivity to alcohol, development and consequences of fetal alcohol syndrome, characteristics and negative effects of alcoholic families, and prevention and treatment of problems in alcoholic and nonalcoholic family members. There is also a chapter on ethical and public policy issues such as child abuse and health insurance for treatment. Intended to serve as a catalyst for further examination into the needs and problems of COAs. References.

19.    Windle, Michael, and John S. Searles, eds. **Children of Alcoholics: Critical Perspectives.** New York: Guilford Press, 1990. 244 pp.

Provides critical reviews by well-known researchers and clinicians on the current state of knowledge regarding children of alcoholics. The reviews cover a broad range of topics related to COAs: prevalence studies of alcoholism among COAs, biochemical markers for alcoholism, neuropsychological and neurophysiological characteristics of COAs, behavior genetic research and risk for alcoholism among COAs, temperament and personality attributes, family factors and adjustment, and prevention and treatment approaches. Each review examines the methodologies and conclusions, as well as strengths and weaknesses, of existing research literature and identifies future research needs. The final chapter discusses several common themes--such as the need for biopsychosocial models integrating environmental and genetic factors--for future research on COAs and suggests a life-span developmental perspective for guiding such research. This book provides an excellent, balanced overview of current theory and treatment approaches for COAs; it is intended for researchers, treatment personnel, educators, and policymakers. References, index.

20.     Woodside, Migs. **Children of Alcoholics.** Albany: New
        York State Division of Alcoholism and Alcohol
        Abuse, 1982. 50 pp.

        Presents the findings of a major report by the New
York State Heroin and Alcohol Abuse Study on the
problems and needs of children of alcoholics. Begins with a
review of the contemporary research literature followed by
statistics on the number of COAs in New York and a
survey of programs providing services for COAs within the
state. There is a detailed chapter on important issues such
as child abuse, treatment services for COAs, and research,
and recommendations are suggested to deal with these
issues more effectively. This report serves as an important
overview and a basic foundation for further study of the
needs of COAs. References, bibliography.

### Journal Articles

21.     Bennett, Linda A., Steven J. Wolin, and David Reiss.
        "Cognitive, Behavioral, and Emotional Problems
        Among School-Age Children of Alcoholic Parents."
        *American Journal of Psychiatry* 145(1988): 185-90.

        Discusses results of a study comparing cognitive,
behavioral, and emotional functioning of school-age
children of alcoholics with children of nonalcoholic
parents. Data on children and their parents was gathered
by a variety of instruments including the Michigan
Alcoholism Screening Test, the Wechsler Intelligence Scale
for Children-Revised, and the Piers-Harris Children's Self-
Concept Scale. In addition parents were interviewed about
their alcohol use and were asked to complete separate
assessments of their children's behavior. Analysis of the
data showed that children of alcoholics functioned less
well than the control group, especially in the cognitive and
emotional areas. References.

22.    Brown, Sandra A., Vicki A. Creamer, and Barbara A.
       Stetson. "Adolescent Alcohol Expectancies in
       Relation to Personal and Parental Drinking
       Patterns." *Journal of Abnormal Psychology* 96(1987):
       117-21.

       Examines the relationship of expectations of positive
effects of alcohol to drinking patterns of adolescents. The
study compared alcohol expectancies of adolescent alcohol
abusers in treatment to a control group of nonabusing
adolescents using the Alcohol Expectancy Questionnaire. In
addition, parents of the subjects were included in the
study, and subjects were grouped according to personal
alcohol use as well as family history of abuse. Results
indicated that adolescent alcohol abusers expected
significantly more positive reinforcement from alcohol use
than did nonabusers. Also, adolescents with an alcohol-
abusing parent reported expecting more cognitive and motor
enhancement from drinking than did adolescents from
nonabusing families. Findings suggest that adolescents may
be at risk for alcohol problems because of parental
drinking behavior and also because of acquired expectations
regarding alcohol's effects. References.

23.    Clair, David, and Myles Genest. "Variables
       Associated With the Adjustment of Offspring of
       Alcoholic Fathers." *Journal of Studies on Alcohol*
       48(1987): 345-55.

       Examines the role of moderator variables (family
environment, social support, and coping behaviors) in the
adjustment of children of alcoholics. A group of young
adult children of alcoholic fathers and a comparison group
of children of nonalcoholics were assessed retrospectively
regarding problem situations when they were 13-18 years of
age. Their present adjustment was also measured using the
Depression-Proneness Rating Scale and the Tennessee Self-
Concept Scale. Results confirmed that COAs did perceive
their families as more dysfunctional and that they received
less support and engaged in more avoidance behaviors than

the comparison group. Although the COAs reported more proneness to depression, they did not differ from the comparison group on levels of self-esteem, and many COAs were functioning as well as, or better than, the average level of comparison subjects. Findings indicate that moderator variables play an important role in the variability of adjustment by COAs. References.

24.     Dinning, W. David, and Leo A. Berk. "The Children of Alcoholics Screening Test: Relationship to Sex, Family Environment, and Social Adjustment in Adolescents." *Journal of Clinical Psychology* 45(1989): 335-39.

Examines the relationship of the Children of Alcoholics Screening Test (CAST) to measures of family environment and social maladjustment in adolescents. Findings showed the CAST to be related significantly to high family conflict, low family cohesion, and low family support but not to family expressiveness or social maladjustment. Also, scores between males and females were found to differ significantly. References.

25.     Holden, Matthew G., Sandra A. Brown, and Miriam A. Mott. "Social Support Network of Adolescents: Relation to Family Alcohol Abuse." *American Journal of Drug and Alcohol Abuse* 14(1988): 487-98.

Describes a research project to determine relationship between adolescent social functioning, adolescent drinking, and parental alcohol abuse. The data showed that alcohol-abusing teenagers and teenagers from alcoholic families had fewer social supports than nonabusing teenagers from nonalcoholic families. Reduced social supports in combination with stressful life events were felt to enhance the risk of COAs for a variety of emotional, behavioral, and physical problems. References.

26.    Jacob,    Theodore,    and    Kenneth    Leonard.
       "Psychosocial Functioning in Children of Alcoholic
       Fathers, Depressed Fathers and Control Fathers."
       *Journal of Studies on Alcohol* 47(1986): 373-80.

Examines psychological problems among children of
alcoholic fathers as compared to children of depressed (but
not alcoholic) fathers and children of social drinking (not
depressed) fathers. All families in the study contained a
mother who was not diagnosed with alcoholism or major
mental disorder. None of the participating family members
was involved in treatment at the time of the study.
Children aged 10-18 were assessed by their parents using
the Child Behavior Checklist and by their teachers using
two instruments to evaluate learning disorders and behavior
problems. Results showed that children of alcoholic and
depressed fathers exhibited more behavior problems than
children of controls. However, severe levels of impairment
were present only in a minority of these families.
References.

27.    Johnson, S., K.E. Leonard, and T. Jacob. "Drinking,
       Drinking Styles and Drug Use in Children of
       Alcoholics, Depressives and Controls." *Journal of
       Studies on Alcohol* 50(1989): 427-31.

Compares alcohol and drug use among adolescent
children of alcoholic, depressed, and normal fathers. Based
on sample population used by Jacob and Leonard (see item
26 above). No significant differences were found between
COAs    and    the    other    groups    in    terms    of    alcohol
consumption, attitudes toward use, and drinking behaviors.
However, COAs were found to exhibit more drug-using
behavior. Researchers suggested that alcohol problem
behaviors may not show up in adolescence due to relative
inaccessibility of alcohol as well as other mitigating family
factors. Parental alcoholism may also increase general risk
for substance abuse among offspring rather than increased
risk for specific substances. References.

28.    Marcus, Adrienne M. "Academic Achievement in
       Elementary School Children of Alcoholic Mothers."
       *Journal of Clinical Psychology* 42(1986): 372-76.

       Describes a study comparing academic achievement
of elementary school-aged children who have alcoholic
mothers with a group of similar children of nonalcoholic
mothers. Mothers for both groups were primarily white,
well-educated, and middle class, and children in both
groups were similar in age, grade level, number of siblings,
and prior grade retention. Findings showed that the
children of alcoholic mothers scored consistently lower
than the control group in academic performance as
measured by the Peabody Individual Achievement Test.
These results replicated findings of an earlier study with
lower-class COAs. References.

29.    Marcus, Adrienne M., and Suzanne Tisne.
       "Perception of Maternal Behavior by Elementary
       School Children of Alcoholic Mothers." *International
       Journal of the Addictions* 22(1987): 543-55.

       Discusses findings of a study comparing perceptions
of maternal behavior by young children of alcoholic parents
with a control group of children from nonalcoholic families.
Children's perceptions were measured in three areas:
acceptance versus rejection, psychological autonomy versus
psychological control, and firm control versus lax control.
Results indicated that COAs perceived their mothers as
equally accepting and psychologically controlling as did the
control group; however, COAs also perceived the use of
maternal guilt as a means of control to a greater extent
than did controls. Several possible factors related to these
perceptions are discussed, focusing on the dynamics of the
alcoholic family. References.

30.    Murray, John B. "Psychologists and Children of
       Alcoholic Parents." *Psychological Reports* 64(1989):
       859-79.

Reviews the research literature on children of alcoholics to determine if evidence supports the picture of COAs as physically, emotionally, socially, and academically vulnerable. Includes literature on fetal alcohol syndrome as well as research on pre-school through adult populations, examining such factors as cognitive functioning, social adequacy, family roles, and psychiatric disorder. Briefly looks at treatment approaches including group therapy, Al-Anon and Alateen, and art therapy. References.

31.     Pandina, Robert J., and Valerie Johnson. "Familial Drinking History as a Predictor of Alcohol and Drug Consumption Among Adolescent Children." *Journal of Studies on Alcohol* 50(1989): 245-53.

Presents data from a longitudinal study of teenagers and young adults to describe early differences in alcohol and drug use patterns of children from families with a positive history of alcoholism and those without such a background. Correlation between positive family history of alcoholism and early onset of problem drinking was found to be relatively weak. Other factors that may increase risk of alcohol problems are identified. References.

32.     Plant, Martin A., Jim Orford, and Marcus Grant. "The Effects on Children and Adolescents of Parents' Excessive Drinking: An International Review." *Public Health Reports* 104(1989): 433-42.

Reviews research on the effects during childhood, adolescence, and adulthood of having a parent with an alcohol problem. The research cited is international in scope; most was published in the United States and eastern Europe from the 1950s to the mid-1980s. Includes studies dealing with psychological disturbance, intelligence and school performance, social adjustment, behavioral problems, suicide, family problems, and substance abuse. References.

33.    "Psychosocial   Characteristics   of   Children   of
       Alcoholics [Symposium]." *British Journal of Addiction*
       83(1988): 783-857.

       Includes   eight   papers   presented   by   noted
researchers at a 1987 meeting sponsored by the National
Institute  on  Alcohol  Abuse  and  Alcoholism  and  the
American  Research  Society  on  Alcoholism.  The  papers
include  a  review  of  the  existing  research  literature  on
children and adult children of alcoholics as well as a look
at  the  contemporary  grassroots  movement  to  provide
awareness and services to meet the needs of COAs. Several
specific  studies  are  described,  covering  such  topics  as
personality disorders in COAs, cognitive and psychomotor
characteristics  of  ACOAs,  family  rituals  as  protective
mechanisms  for  COAs,  affective  disorders  and  cognitive
functioning  in  young  COAs,  and  an  examination  of  home
and social environments of COAs. References.

34.    Roosa, Mark W., Leah K. Gensheimer, Jerome L.
       Short, Tim S. Ayers, and Rita Shell. "A Preventive
       Intervention  for  Children  in  Alcoholic  Families:
       Results of a Pilot Study." *Family Relations* 38(1989):
       295-300.

       Reviews  the  literature  on  prevention  programming
for children of alcoholics and describes the development
and evaluation of a school-based program for COAs aged 9-
13.  The  curriculum  focused  on  stress  management  and
alcohol awareness and included coping strategies and self-
esteem  enhancement.  The  pilot  study  involved  primarily
low-income  students  from  three  inner  city  schools.
Recruitment  was  voluntary  (with  parental  approval),  and
response was higher than expected. One of the test schools
also included a personal trainer component, which matched
individual students to adults who helped to provide social
support,  reinforcement,  and  positive  role  models.  Results  of
the  study  indicated  that  students  and  school  personnel
rated  the  program  highly  and  that  the  personal  trainer

component could be implemented at relatively low cost.
References.

35.     Roosa, Mark W., Irwin N. Sandler, Janette Beals,
        and Jerome L. Short. "Risk Status of Adolescent
        Children of Problem-Drinking Parents." *American
        Journal of Community Psychology* 16(1988): 225-39.

        Presents the results of a study to assess risk of
children of alcoholics for developing psychological or
substance abuse disorders. Results showed that COAs were
more likely than children in the general population to
suffer from certain psychological problems; however, within
self-help groups, children of nonalcoholics with different
symptomology were equally at risk. The authors argue for
the development and implementation of prevention programs
to identify at-risk children as early as possible.
References.

36.     Roosa, Mark W., Irwin N. Sandler, Mary Gehring,
        Janette Beals, and Laurel Cappo. "The Children of
        Alcoholics Life-Events Schedule: A Stress Scale for
        Children of Alcohol-Abusing Parents." *Journal of
        Studies on Alcohol* 49(1988): 422-29.

        Describes the development of the Children of
Alcoholics Life-Events Schedule (COALES) to help predict
those COAs most at risk for mental health problems.
Includes a copy of the questionnaire and information about
its reliability and validity. References.

37.     "Symposium: The Genetics of Alcoholism."
        *Alcoholism: Clinical and Experimental Research*
        12(1988): 457-505.

        Presents six research studies examining various
aspects of the role of genetic factors in the etiology of
alcoholism. Several studies focus specifically on children of
alcoholics, covering topics such as familial transmission of
alcoholism, differential effects of alcohol consumption on

sons of alcoholics, and frequency of psychiatric disorder in children of alcoholics. References.

38.    Tarter, Ralph E., Theodore Jacob, and Deborah A. Bremer. "Cognitive Status of Sons of Alcoholic Men." *Alcoholism: Clinical and Experimental Research* 13(1989): 232-34.

Compares cognitive functioning of sons of alcoholic fathers to sons of normal and depressed fathers. All fathers were married and living in the community, and none were in treatment for alcohol problems. Sons were aged 8-17 years and were administered a battery of neuropsychological tests. Results did not indicate a generalized cognitive impairment in sons of community dwelling alcoholic men; however, some deficits were found in areas related to planning ability and impulse control. Impairment in these processes may be associated with increased risk for alcoholism and may indicate an anterior cerebral dysfunction. References.

39.    Wallace, John. "Children of Alcoholics: A Population at Risk." *Alcoholism Treatment Quarterly* 4(Fall 1987): 13-30.

Reviews current knowledge and research needs on the physiological, psychological, and social problems frequently suffered by children of alcoholics. Explores genetic predisposition to alcoholism as well as the negative effects of alcohol toxicity on the developing fetus. References.

40.    West, Melissa O., and Ronald J. Prinz. "Parental Alcoholism and Childhood Psychopathology." *Psychological Bulletin* 102(1987): 204-18.

Reviews research literature on the effects of parental alcoholism on childhood psychopathology. Examines findings of studies covering eight areas of outcome:

hyperactivity and conduct disorder; substance abuse, delinquency, and truancy; cognitive functioning; social inadequacy; physical health problems; anxiety and depressive symptoms; physical abuse; and dysfunctional family interactions. Although findings as a whole support the contention that parental alcoholism is related to increased childhood psychopathology, neither all nor a majority of COAs have suffered from such disorders. The authors discuss some of the methodological problems contained in this research and offer suggestions for improving research techniques in the future. References.

41.     Williams, Carol N. "Child Care Practices in Alcoholic Families: Findings from a Neighborhood Detoxification Program." *Alcohol Health and Research World* 11(Summer 1987): 74-77, 94.

Reports findings of a study that compared child care practices and prevalence of abuse and neglect among alcoholic families. Discovered that families with alcoholic fathers showed the greatest stability and most competent child care, while families with two alcoholic parents had the least competent child care and were most likely to abuse and neglect their children. Families with alcoholic mothers had the least financial resources and the least stability but provided better care than the two-alcoholic parent families. The author suggests that families with an alcoholic mother would benefit most from comprehensive family treatment interventions. References.

42.     Woodside, Migs. "Children of Alcoholics: Helping a Vulnerable Group." *Public Health Reports* 103(1988): 643-48.

Presents a brief overview of research on children of alcoholics, including studies of fetal alcohol syndrome, health problems, and psychological problems. Describes life in an alcoholic family and suggests ways that health professionals can identify and respond to the needs and problems of COAs. References.

See also: 88, 114, 123, 135, 139, 175, 196.

## 3. FAMILY ISSUES

### Books and Pamphlets

This chapter covers literature on a variety of issues pertaining to children of alcoholics in the family setting. Topics include characteristics, family roles, and coping skills of COAs, experiences and childhood development of COAs, and information about alcoholism as a family disease. Most of the items are intended to increase understanding and awareness of the effects of parental alcoholism on children.

43.    Abbott, Stephanie. **Family Album: Alcoholism, Co-Dependence, and Other Addictions.** Seattle: National Foundation for Alcoholism Communications, 1987. 83 pp.

Collection of articles originally published in **Alcoholism and Addiction Magazine** from 1979 to 1987. The articles are directed at family members who are coping with an alcoholic spouse or parent. Each piece focuses on a particular problem commonly associated with family alcoholism, such as dealing with anger, detaching from the alcoholic, and sexual relations, and offers brief suggestions for handling these issues. Separate sections deal specifically with problems suffered by adult children of alcoholics and with problems that may be encountered in family treatment.

44.    Ackerman, Robert J., and Susan E. Pickering.
       **Abused No More: Recovery for Women from Abusive
       or Co-Dependent Relationships.** Blue Ridge Summit,
       PA: TAB Books, 1989. 201 pp.

Offers practical advice to help women who are
physically, sexually, or emotionally abused by their
partners. Uses personal histories to describe the contexts
and effects of abuse, including the role of alcohol in
abusive behavior. Also examines reasons why women often
stay in abusive relationships, touching on the influence of
childhood family patterns that may have been physically
abusive, alcoholic, or both. There is a very useful chapter
devoted to getting help for children from abusive families
(whether or not the children themselves are being
battered); much of this chapter focuses on the special
problems of children of alcoholics, who need the support of
a healthy, stable nonalcoholic parent. Bibliography.

45.    Anderson, Peggy K. **Coming Home: Adult Children of
       Alcoholics.** Seattle: Glen Abbey Books, 1988. 129 pp.

Tells the story of two young children whose
alcoholic father goes into treatment. Focuses on the
children's loss of trust in family relationships and describes
their difficulties with school and friends as a result of
their family problem. This book is announced as the first
of the Mending Memories series, which are intended to
help adult children deal with the feelings and experiences
of growing up in an alcoholic home. However, the text,
illustrations, and large print are appropriate for an
audience aged 8-14 years. A special "child's page" is
included at the end to advise children to confide feelings
and anxieties about parental alcoholism to an adult
(teacher, friend, relative) they can trust. There is a brief
list of organizations for help as well as a book list of
titles primarily for adult children.

46.     Brooks, Cathleen. **The Secret Everyone Knows.** San Diego: Operation Cork, 1981. 40 pp.

Presents a sensitive and insightful discussion of the effects of parental alcoholism on the thoughts, feelings, and behaviors of children. Also includes basic information about the disease aspects of alcoholism and suggests strategies and resources for coping with alcohol problems in the family.

47.     **Children of Alcoholics.** South Deerfield, MA: Channing L. Bete Co., 1987. 15 pp.

Uses line drawings to help illustrate many of the consequences of growing up with an alcoholic parent. Describes some of the coping skills that children develop to deal with alcoholic parents and also demonstrates the links that may exist from childhood experiences to adult emotional development. Warns of the risks to COAs of developing addictive behaviors and includes a brief list of sources for help. The text is concise and easy to understand and would be appropriate for young teens through adults.

48.     **Children of Alcoholics: The Truth Behind Hard Love.** Madison: Wisconsin Clearinghouse, 1988. 2 pp.

Briefly summarizes the emotional and behavioral traits common to many children of alcoholics. Describes several unique aspects of a COA's childhood, including trauma, development of survival skills, repression of feelings, and loss of trust. Concludes with a short list of resources for information about COAs or recovery groups and an equally short list of titles for further reading (all of which focus on adult children). Suitable for teens or adults.

49.     Deutsch,     Charles.     **Children     of     Alcoholics:**
        **Understanding and Helping.** Deerfield Beach, FL:
        Health Communications, 1983. 12 pp.

Examines the effects of parental alcoholism on the
emotional development of children. Identifies defensive
roles that children adopt in order to cope with an alcoholic
family situation and includes suggestions to help parents,
school personnel, or other concerned adults recognize and
deal with children of alcoholics.

50.     Deutsch, Charles. **When Parents Drink Too Much,**
        **You Can Still Find Your Way.** New York: Children
        of Alcoholics Foundation, 1986. 3 pp.

Offers practical advice to teenagers and pre-teens
about coping with parental alcoholism. Includes a short quiz
to test knowledge of alcoholism and provides suggestions
for getting more information and help. Identifies possible
persons to talk to about family alcoholism, such as
teachers, other relatives, or family doctor, and concludes
with separate reading lists for younger children and
teenagers. Bibliography.

51.     Dolmetsch, Paul, and Gail Mauricette, eds. **Teens**
        **Talk About Alcohol and Alcoholism.** Garden City,
        NY: Dolphin/Doubleday, 1987. 125 pp.

Written for children living in alcoholic families by a
group of eighth-grade students in Vermont. Provides an
excellent, unbiased, easy-to-understand overview of alcohol,
alcoholism, and the effects of alcoholism on family
members, especially children. Describes the effects of
alcohol on the body and behavior and discusses some of
the reasons why people drink. There is also a chapter on
the special problems of being a teenager and why some
teens may use alcohol. Most of the book focuses on
alcoholism--what it is, how it is identified, and how it
affects family life. There are several vignettes describing

family experiences of teenagers with an alcoholic parent, and practical advice is offered to help teenagers cope with the family situation. The book concludes with a helpful chapter on recovery, which discusses what to expect from parental recovery, how to help a parent get treatment, and the importance of therapy for all family members. This book would be useful for parents and teachers as well as teenagers. Includes a section of short book reviews done by the students.

52. FitzGerald, Kathleen W. Alcoholism: **The Genetic Inheritance.** New York: Doubleday, 1988. 248 pp.

Defines alcoholism as a disease characterized by genetic susceptibility that leads to physical dependence on alcohol. Emphasizes the biological rather than environmental influences on the etiology of alcoholism and identifies the biochemical markers that may be responsible for the development of tolerance and addiction to alcohol. Describes the progression of the disease as it affects the alcoholic and the other members of the family and includes guidelines to help family or significant others motivate an alcoholic into treatment. There is one chapter devoted specifically to the effects of parental alcoholism on children, describing the various roles children may adopt to cope with the domestic situation. The book is intended for alcoholics and family members and provides several brief case histories to illustrate the stages of alcoholic behavior. Sources for the statistics used are not cited. The appendix contains six helpful self-tests to identify possible chemical dependency in an individual or a family. Glossary, bibliography, index.

53. Hammond, Mary, and Lynnann Chestnut. **My Mom Doesn't Look Like an Alcoholic.** Deerfield Beach, FL: Health Communications, 1984. 36 pp.

Presents a child's perspective of what it is like to live with an alcoholic parent. Describes feelings of insecurity, anger, fear, isolation, and overresponsiblity that many young children experience in similar situations and contrasts these with the positive changes in family relations that can occur when a parent achieves sobriety. Gives only a brief explanation of alcoholism as a disease, emphasizing that children are not to blame for its development or consequences. Suitable for children aged 9- 12 or may be used by parents or counselors with individual children or in groups. Illustrations.

54.     Jance, Judith A. **Welcome Home: A Child's View of Family Alcoholism.** Illustrated by Marina Megale. Children's Safety Series, book 7. Edmonds, WA: Charles Franklin Press, 1986. 30 pp.

Offers helpful information for children (ages 8-12) who live with an alcoholic parent. Uses the fictional story of a young boy whose father is alcoholic to demonstrate how alcoholism may affect children--through family violence, erratic parental behavior, embarrassment, confusion, and guilt. Emphasizes that alcoholism is a disease that can neither be caused nor controlled by children's behaviors and suggests ways for children to seek help in coping with an alcoholic parent. Includes a special introduction for parents or other concerned adults. Illustrations, bibliography.

55.     **Learn About Children of Alcoholics.** Center City, MN: Hazelden, 1985. 15 pp.

Briefly describes some of the problems of growing up in an alcoholic family, including abuse, neglect, shame, and inability to express feelings. Provides a short annotated list of organizations to contact for help. Concise and easy to read. Part of a series for general readers (young teens through adults) who have very little knowledge about alcohol or drug abuse.

56.     Leiner, Katherine. **Something's Wrong in My House**.
        New York: Franklin Watts, 1988. 63 pp.

        Presents the stories of elementary through high
school-aged children who have an alcoholic parent. The
stories are told by children from a wide range of ethnic
and socioeconomic backgrounds, and they depict a variety
of experiences including neglect, family violence, and
delinquent behavior. Many of the stories demonstrate some
effective resources for coping with parental alcoholism,
such as Alateen, Girls Clubs, and school personnel. Each
story is illustrated with photographs of the children
themselves at home, at school, or with family or friends.
The text is candid but sensitive and is designed to let
children of alcoholics know that many other children have
problems similar to theirs. There is a short reading list as
well as a list of organizations to contact for help.

57.     Leite, Evelyn, and Pamela Espeland. **Different Like
        Me: A Book for Teens Who Worry About Their
        Parents' Use of Alcohol/Drugs**. Minneapolis: Johnson
        Institute, 1987. 110 pp.

        Describes what it is like for teenagers who live
with an alcoholic or drug abusing parent. Provides basic
information about the disease of chemical dependency and
offers practical suggestions to help teens cope with the
family situation. Intersperses vignettes describing teens'
family experiences with facts, statistics, and warning signs
of chemical dependence. Includes a list of resources for
help.

58.     McFarland, Rhoda. **Coping with Substance Abuse**.
        New York: Rosen Publishing Group, 1987. 145 pp.

        Written to help teenagers understand the disease of
alcoholism and its effects on the individual and the family.
Includes chapters on coping with an alcoholic parent,
coping with drug abusing siblings, and coping with friends
who drink and use drugs. Describes the process of

intervention to help motivate family members into treatment and includes a list of organizations for further information and help. Also discusses symptoms and consequences of teenage chemical dependency and offers suggestions for getting help. Index.

59.    Mills, Dixie, and Charles Deutsch. **Happy Hill Farm.** Somerville, MA: CASPAR Alcohol Education Program, n.d. 11 pp.

Pamphlet written to accompany the **Decisions About Drinking** curriculum (see item 98). Tells the story of Farmer Gray, whose alcoholism begins to affect the animals on his farm. A variety of reactions, from denial to guilt and anger, are expressed by the animals, who finally bring the problem to the attention of a concerned veterinarian. The goal of the text is to help young children clarify their own feelings toward an alcoholic parent and to let them know that they are not to blame for the alcoholic's behavior. Suitable for classroom discussion or group work with COAs. Illustrations.

60.    Nakken, Craig. **The** Addictive **Personality: Roots, Rituals, and Recovery.** Center City, MN: Hazelden, 1988. 116 pp.

Discusses addiction as it relates not only to alcohol and other drugs but also to gambling, sex, eating disorders, and other compulsive behaviors. Defines the process of addiction as an attempt to control mood-altering behaviors and examines the stages of development in this process. There is a section devoted to the problems of growing up in a family with an addictive parent, focusing on how addictive behaviors are often passed on to new generations. This section also includes a discussion of the effects of emotional instability, shame, abuse, and neglect on the development of children. The final section offers a brief outline for recovery from addiction based on developing "natural" relationships and positive rituals (non-addictive behaviors and situations). Index.

61.     Parker, Christina. **Children of Alcoholics: Growing Up Unheard.** Tempe, AZ: Do It Now Foundation, 1986. 2 pp.

Presents a brief overview of the nature and extent of the problems suffered by children of alcoholics. Includes statistics on major problems such as family violence and compulsive behavior (no references are given). Briefly describes several emotional problems--including guilt, anxiety, and depression--and identifies common roles that COAs may adopt to cope within the family. Provides practical suggestions for getting help. Appropriate for adolescents or adults, as well as therapists and educators who want basic, concise information on these problems.

62.     Perez, Joseph F. **Coping Within the Alcoholic Family.** Muncie, IN: Accelerated Development Inc., 1986. 178 pp.

Uses case histories to illustrate the dynamics at work within an alcoholic family. Discusses the role of the enabler (usually the spouse) in maintaining the alcoholic family system and presents examples from family therapy sessions that led to positive change in family behaviors. There are two parts of the text that focus on children of alcoholics. Part II describes some common characteristics of alcoholics--such as impulsivity and low tolerance for frustration--and how these affect family relationships. There are also several case reports by alcoholics who describe their perceptions of how their alcoholism affected their children. In part III some common characteristics of children of alcoholics are identified, such as inability to trust, emotional distancing, and unreliability. In addition, there is a separate section that deals with the special problems that are generated in single parent families with alcoholism. The book concludes with a helpful discussion of do's and dont's for nondrinking family members. Although written especially for alcoholics, spouses, and adult or teenage children of alcoholics, the book would also be useful to family therapists who frequently deal with alcohol problems. Bibliography.

63.     Porterfield, Kay M. Coping With an Alcoholic Parent. New York: Rosen Publishing Group, 1985. 134 pp.

Part of the Coping series designed to help teenagers deal with serious personal and family problems. Provides some basic information about alcoholism and its warning signs and explores the feelings and behaviors that teens often experience from living with an alcoholic parent. Offers advice for teens to reach out for help, especially through Alateen. Also discusses what changes to expect in the family if an alcoholic parent becomes sober and concludes with a chapter that addresses a teen's possible fear of becoming alcoholic. There is a suggested reading list as well as a list of organizations to contact for further information or help. Provides a sensitive yet straightforward treatment of a delicate issue.

64.     The Real Story! COA Guide: Understanding the Alcoholic Family. Troy, MI: Performance Resource Press, n.d. 15 pp.

Uses comic book format to illustrate the different roles of family members in an alcoholic family. Also briefly describes the process of intervention (through an employee assistance program) and steps toward family recovery. Concludes with a warning checklist to help parents recognize signs of alcohol or other drug use in their children. Although the format of the text seems geared toward a teenaged audience, the writing is more appropriate for adult children and parents. There is a short list of resource organizations. Bibliography.

65.    Rosenberg, Maxine B. **Not My Family: Sharing the Truth About Alcoholism.** New York: Bradbury Press, 1988. 97 pp.

Contains brief descriptions of childhood experiences with an alcoholic parent. There are fourteen separate stories told by young children and adults who grew up in alcoholic homes. Most stories do not offer definite guidelines for dealing with parental alcoholism, but they do provide examples of alcoholic behavior and illustrate successful methods of coping in similar situations. There is also a list of organizations for sources of help. The text would be suitable for adolescents as well as adult COAs and for therapists working with these populations. Bibliography, index.

66.    Roy, Maria. **Children in the Crossfire: Violence in the Home--How Does It Affect Our Children?** Deerfield Beach, FL: Health Communications, 1988. 211 pp.

Describes the psychological damage suffered by women and children who are victims of family violence. Reviews the prevalence of spouse and child abuse-- including physical and sexual abuse and neglect--and discusses factors associated with its manifestation and perpetuation. There are several case histories of teenagers and adults that illustrate the link between alcohol and other drug abuse and domestic violence. The stories also demonstrate how children may turn to alcohol or other drugs as a reaction to the family situation. The text concludes with guidelines and a list of organizations to help individuals who want to escape from family violence. Suitable for counselors, educators, adults, and older teens. References, bibliography.

67.    Ryerson, Eric. **When Your Parent Drinks Too Much: A Book for Teenagers.** New York: Facts on File Publications, 1985. 125 pp.

Designed to provide help for teenagers living with an alcoholic parent. Includes basic information on the disease of alcoholism, warning signs, effects on family members, and practical advice for coping with the situation. Also discusses some of the problems faced by a newly-sober parent and offers suggestions for providing family support. Appendixes provide information on dealing with special crises, such as family violence, drunk driving, and fires, as well as a resource list of organizations (which needs to be updated and expanded). Index.

68.     Seixas, Judith S. **Living With a Parent Who Drinks Too Much.** New York: Greenwillow Books, 1979. 116 pp.

Provides basic information for children of alcoholics about the disease of alcoholism and its effects on the alcoholic and on family behaviors and relationships. Describes the warning signs of alcoholism and talks about some of the problems that may occur in the family when a parent is recovering from this disease. Suggests practical ways that children can cope with parental alcoholism and also discusses the special risks of alcohol use for COAs. Suitable for young teens or pre-teens.

69.     Shiromoto, Frank N., and Edgar F. Soren. **Drugs and Drinks: Painful Questions. How Substance Abusers and Their Loved Ones Ask for Help.** Monterey, CA: Choices Press, 1988. 135 pp.

Uses a question-and-answer format to present information about alcoholism and other drug abuse. Provides brief descriptions of the harmful effects and dependency potential for the main drugs of abuse, including alcohol. The bulk of the text is divided into sections for alcohol and drug users, spouses and partners of users, minor children of users, adult children, and parents of users. The sections for minor and adult children address such concerns as how to get help for addicted parents and whether alcoholism or drug dependence can be inherited. There are two tests included to help chemical users and other family members determine whether an alcohol or drug problem exists. This book is intended for all adult family members and children from junior high through high school age. The appendixes include lists of national organizations and state agencies to contact for further information or help with an alcohol or drug problem as well as a list of toll-free information numbers. Glossary, bibliography.

70.    Wegscheider, Sharon. **The Family Trap...No One Escapes from a Chemically Dependent Family**. 2d ed. Rapid City, MN: Nurturing Networks, 1979. 17 pp.

Provides an excellent description of the various survival roles--enabler, hero, scapegoat, lost child, and mascot--commonly adopted by members of a chemically dependent family. Useful for family members and therapists.

71.    Wegscheider-Cruse, Sharon, and Richard W. Esterly, eds. **Alcoholism and the Family: A Book of Readings**. Wernersville, PA: Caron Institute, 1985. 70 pp.

Presentations from the 1984 National Conference on Alcoholism and the Family. Section I focuses on alcoholism as a family illness and defines codependency in terms of behaviors or roles developed by family members to cope with a dysfunctional family situation. There are articles dealing specifically with the needs of children of alcoholics (including adult children) and also the relationship of alcoholism to domestic violence. Section II describes particular techniques and approaches for therapists dealing with alcoholic families. In section III special issues related to recovery and spirituality within the family are discussed. These articles represent the experience and opinions of several well-known alcohol practitioners.

Journal Articles

72.    Ackerman, Robert J. "Stress in the Addicted Family:
       How We Cope Makes the Difference." *Focus on
       Chemically Dependent Families* 11(Aug.-Sept. 1988):
       13.

Describes some of the ways in which stress can
affect members of alcoholic families. Discusses why some
children and adults may react more positively to the stress
of an alcoholic family and identifies several factors that
can lead to the development of healthy coping skills.

73.    Berlin, Richard, Ruth B. Davis, and Alan Orenstein.
       "Adaptive and Reactive Distancing Among
       Adolescents from Alcoholic Families." *Adolescence*
       23(1988): 577-84.

Describes the difficulties which adolescent children
of alcoholics may experience in separating emotionally
and/or physically from their families. Differentiates
between reactive and adaptive distancing (from family) and
relates the distancing process to the types of fantasies
that children may develop from living in an alcoholic
family. References.

74.    Lerner, Rokelle. "Developmental Obstacles in the
       Alcoholic Family--Reclaiming the Child's Spirit."
       *Focus on Family and Chemical Dependency* 9(Nov.-
       Dec. 1986): 12-13, 19.

Discusses the "developmental sabotage" that often
happens with children in alcoholic families. Describes the
problems that may occur at different stages to prevent
proper development and provides examples of the behaviors
that may result. Puts special emphasis on "boundary
invasion"--when a child is prevented from discovering
personal boundaries and what constitutes appropriate or
inappropriate behavior.

75.    Lynch, Brian. "Double Dose of Guilt--Child Sexual Abuse in the Alcoholic Family." *Focus on Family and Chemical Dependency* 9(Nov.-Dec. 1986): 26-27, 30.

Discusses the relationship between child sexual abuse and parental alcoholism. Explains why alcoholics sometimes turn to children as sexual partners and describes the children's feelings of shame, guilt, and responsibility.

76.    Norton, Jamie H. "Common Lessons from Addicted Family Systems: Teach Your Children Well." *Focus on Family and Chemical Dependency* 9(July-Aug. 1986): 10-12, 35.

Describes a program designed for youthful substance abusers, which was offered in both correctional facilities and schools. Many of the participants came from families with alcohol or drug abusing parents, and program personnel identified a number of common threads among the COAs. These characteristics and behaviors are discussed in detail and include chronic stress response, chronic grief, low self-image, and poor relationship and communication skills.

77.    Nuckols, Cardwell C. "Insight on the Oldest Child." *Focus on Family and Chemical Dependency* 7(Jan.-Feb. 1984): 34-35.

Describes the hero role often assumed by the oldest child in an alcoholic family. Discusses how and why this role evolves and gives examples of consequent behaviors and feelings.

See also: 10, 16, 83, 87, 90, 93, 94, 105, 155, 168, 170, 198, 209, 211, 212, 246, 310.

## 4. TREATMENT

### Books and Pamphlets

The materials described in this chapter are intended primarily for an audience of trained professionals-- counselors, family therapists, educators, health care workers. Some of the items are meant for use by personnel who are experienced in working with members of addictive families. Other materials are designed to help professionals identify and deal effectively with COAs and family members among their client populations. Also included are curricula and teacher training materials that have components specifically designed to help identify and work with children of alcoholics in the school setting. Literature on self-help approaches and other recovery issues not dealt with in a professional therapeutic setting is covered in chapter five, **Children: Recovery.**

78. **Babes Kids.** Southfield, MI: Babes World, 1987. 155 pp. (leader's manual)

Presents a twelve-session activity-based program for use in treatment settings with children of alcoholic or drug abusing families. Uses puppets and stories to help children understand the roles and dynamics of chemically dependent families. Also provides basic information about chemical dependence and its effects on the individual and helps children to recognize and deal with their feelings about themselves, family members, and alcohol and drug use. The leader's manual provides information for therapists about the stages of child development, recognizing children of alcoholics, and designing groups for young COAs, as well as outlines of the session activities. Appendixes contain sample letters to solicit parent and school involvement as well as family assessment forms. In addition to the manual, the set includes ten puppets. This is a component of the **Basic Babes** substance abuse prevention program for use with children ages 3-12. Training in the use of the program is provided by Babes World and is required for purchase.

79.     Barnard, Charles P. **Families with an Alcoholic Member: The Invisible Patient.** New York: Human Sciences Press, 1990. 173 pp.

Describes the effects of parental alcoholism on family relationships and advocates involving the whole family in the recovery process. Uses the family history of an adult child of an alcoholic to illustrate the organizing principles of the alcoholic family, including special family roles, boundary issues, sense of identity, and loyalty. Offers guidelines for addressing these family issues and other problems such as sexual abuse and codependency. Includes an instrument, the Family Inventory of Recovery Elements (FIRE), to help assess issues that need to be addressed in treatment. Written for family therapists and adult family members. References, index.

80.     Bepko, Claudia, with JoAnn Krestan. **The Responsibility Trap: A Blueprint for Treating the Alcoholic Family.** New York: The Free Press, 1985. 261 pp.

Analyzes the behaviors and dynamics within an alcoholic family that reinforce the alcohol-abusing behavior of one or more members. The authors use a family systems perspective to examine dysfunctional patterns of behavior within the family as well as the transmission of alcoholic behavior over generations. They provide guidelines for intervention and treatment of alcoholic families, including a separate chapter on children of alcoholics in the treatment process. They identify the survival roles adopted by children of alcoholics and discuss the problems inherent in role adjustment after parental sobriety is achieved. There is also a brief section on adult children with specific treatment goals focusing on self-experience. This book is well-grounded in family theory and practical experience in alcoholism counseling. It is intended primarily for professional therapists but may be useful for alcoholics, spouses, and adult children. References, bibliography, index.

81.    Brennan, Gale P. **I Know They Love Me Anyway....** Illustrated by Meri H. Berghauer. Milwaukee: De Paul Rehabilitation Hospital, 1986. 39 pp.

Written for young school-aged children who may have a poorly developed sense of self-esteem due to parental problems such as alcoholism or financial difficulties. Each set of facing pages is colorfully illustrated, depicting common reactions of children to different family problems--broken promises, isolation, illness, separation. There is an accompanying 36-page guidebook to help teachers, counselors, or parents explore the situations in the text with young children. The book carries a positive tone to help children feel that they are loved despite family troubles. Illustrations.

82.    Campidilli, Patti. **Children from Alcoholic Families: A Resource and Curriculum Guide.** Ames, IA: Youth and Shelter Services, 1985. 45 pp. + appendix.

Outlines a sixteen-session curriculum to help fifth and sixth-graders understand the disease of alcoholism and its impact on families and to provide them with positive coping skills and the means to develop self-confidence and self-esteem. There is background information for educators on the roles and dynamics of alcoholic families as well as a brief discussion of adult child issues that may inhibit teachers' ability to deal effectively with COAs in their classes. Each of the sessions is outlined briefly with main points to be covered, suggestions for presentation, activities and materials. The appendix includes samples of materials and forms that may be reproduced. Bibliography.

83.    **Changing Legacies: Growing Up in an Alcoholic Home.** Deerfield Beach, FL: Health Communications, n.d. 92 pp.

Collection of fifteen articles written by experts known for their work with children of alcoholics. The articles cover a variety of issues related to young children as well as adult children from alcoholic families. Topics include stages of childhood development in COAs, prevention and intervention for pre-school and school-aged COAs, community and school-based services, family roles, abuse in alcoholic families, and characteristics of ACOAs. Although several articles do cite research findings, no complete references are provided. This collection could be helpful to educators, community service providers, and therapists by summarizing the common problems and needs of COAs and offering suggestions for help.

84.    Davis, Ruth B., Patricia D. Johnston, Sally Duncan, and Lena DiCicco. **Learning About Alcohol: The Primary Module of the Decisions About Drinking Curriculum.** Somerville, MA: CASPAR Alcohol Education Program, 1986. 154 pp.

Designed as the first part of the **Decisions About Drinking** curriculum (see item 98) for use with kindergarten through third grade classes. Based on a philosophy of helping children to understand about alcohol, its use, and its effects, in order to make responsible decisions regarding their own use. There are separate modules for each grade level with 4-7 teaching periods outlined for each. Objectives, description of activities, and materials needed are described, and master copies of handouts are provided. The sessions follow a sequence beginning with information and then moving on to attitudes about alcohol and its use, responsible decision making, and alcoholism as a family illness. There is a section of resource material that includes information to help teachers identify and intervene with children who are living in alcoholic families. The producers of the curriculum offer training workshops for teachers and other school personnel who want to use this program in their schools. The CASPAR program has been nationally recognized for its effectiveness in preventing alcohol problems and providing assistance to children of alcoholics.

85.     DiGiovanni, Kathe. **My House is Different.** Center City, MN: Hazelden, 1986. 26 pp.

Uses the fictional story of Joe and his dog Fuzzy to describe the steps of recovery for young children of alcoholics. The story deals with understanding and acceptance of parental alcoholism and building self-esteem in children. Suitable for use by parents, teachers, or counselors with children aged six and older. Illustrations.

86.     Dinklage, Sarah C., Kevin Plummer, and Merrill Kidman. **New Skills: Preventing Alcohol Trouble with Children.** Pawtucket: Rhode Island Youth Guidance Center, 1985. 58 pp. (leader's manual), 46 pp. (children's workbook).

Designed for use in classroom settings, treatment facilities, or social service agencies to help children of alcoholics understand and cope with parental alcoholism. Outlines a two-level education and intervention program for children aged 8-12 years. Level I contains eight sessions focusing on education about alcoholism and awareness of the child's role and needs in an alcoholic family. Level II is optional for programs that have more time and flexibility; it concentrates on using awareness to help children develop a wider range of coping strategies. The package contains a leader's manual that provides general guidelines for facilitating groups and outlines for each of the sessions, covering purpose of the session, materials needed, and suggestions for implementation. There is also a children's workbook (five copies are included in each package) with games, stories, and information to be used in conjunction with the groups. In addition, ten facial expression cards and five mask cards are included to help children identify and express feelings and to illustrate the contrast between feelings and the family roles children often play. There is a short list of resources including books, articles, and audiovisuals.

87.     Duggan, Maureen H. **Mommy Doesn't Live Here Anymore.** Weaverville, NC: Bonnie Brae Publications, 1987. 37 pp.

Describes the emotional effects of a mother's alcoholism from the viewpoint of her ten-year-old daughter. Includes episodes of the mother's passing out and memory loss and her eventual divorce and loss of custody of her children. Provides a sensitive look at the severe trauma suffered by a young child and the slow, painful process of understanding and forgiveness. Intended for use by therapists working with children of alcoholics aged 5-12. There is a separate 14-page pamphlet describing the author's personal and family experiences with alcoholism and including suggested exercises for using these materials in group sessions with young COAs. Illustrations.

88.     Flanzer, Jerry P., and Kinly Sturkie. **Alcohol and Adolescent Abuse: the ALCAN Family Services Treatment Model.** Holmes Beach, FL: Learning Publications, 1987. 85 pp.

Describes the Arkansas Alcohol/Child Abuse Demonstration Project (ALCAN) to study and treat adolescent-abusing families. The goals of the project were to study the relationship between child abuse and alcohol abuse by one or both parents, to provide special training in these areas for social service workers, and to develop a treatment model. The text describes in detail the variables and methodology of the clinical study of 200 adolescent-abusing parents. A separate chapter outlines the treatment program itself, based on a family therapy model including stabilization (of the family situation), assessment, and intervention. The material is well written with numerous tables and a review of the pertinent research literature on alcohol and child abuse as well as family therapy. References.

89.     Fleming, Martin. **Conducting Support Groups for Students Affected by Chemical Dependence: A Guide for Educators and Other Professionals.** Minneapolis: Johnson Institute, 1990. 152 pp.

Offers practical suggestions to help educational personnel (teachers, counselors, school nurses, etc.) establish support groups for children of alcoholics and students involved with (or recovering from) their own substance abuse. Briefly discusses how students may be affected by their own or their parents' substance abuse and identifies important issues to be dealt with in support groups. Provides detailed guidelines for developing a support group, including recruitment of participants, parental involvement, training group leaders, group format and activities. Appendixes include suggested activities, materials, and organizations for further help. Bibliography.

90.     Greenleaf, Jael. **Co-Alcoholic, Para-Alcoholic: Who's Who and What's the Difference?** Denver: MAC Publishing, 1981. 40 pp.

Uses the terms "co-alcoholic" and "para-alcoholic" to identify and distinguish between spouses (or enablers) of alcoholics and children of alcoholics. Defines the co-alcoholic as the aduit partner who assists in maintaining some amount of social and financial equilibrium for the family. This person's role is necessary for the alcoholic to continue to function. Para-alcoholics are described as the children who grow up in an alcoholic family and whose behavior patterns are modeled on the unhealthy roles of their parents. The emphasis of the text is on para-alcoholics and the psychological problems they often develop. Three causes for depression in COAs are discussed, and a number of common behaviors, such as denial and perfectionism, are identified and linked to environmental and emotional factors. The author also outlines several barriers to effective treatment of COAs, including lack of programs specifically designed for COAs, attitudinal barriers in the treatment community, and improper use of assessment techniques. Advocates development of programs that focus on the different needs of spouses and children. Written for the treatment community. Bibliography.

91.     Hammond, Mary L. **Children of Alcoholics in Play Therapy.** Deerfield Beach, FL: Health Communications, 1985. 38 pp.

Describes the use of play as a therapeutic tool with children of alcoholics. Demonstrates how play can be used to provide a safe environment for COAs to express hidden feelings and painful experiences. Offers suggestions to help therapists utilize and interpret play activities of children and includes a chart that illustrates the symptoms and recovery of COAs. References, illustrations.

92.     **It's Elementary: Meeting the Needs of High-Risk Youth in the School Setting.** South Laguna, CA: National Association for Children of Alcoholics, 1989. 29 pp.

Designed to help elementary school personnel-- teachers, counselors, administrators--identify and help students who are living with an alcoholic parent. Presents several short articles written by professional experts on such topics as effects of parental alcoholism on children's school performance, behavioral signs of family alcoholism, and strategies for assisting COAs through school programs and outside resources. Also discusses the special problems experienced by adult COAs who have become educators. There is a very helpful annotated resource list of printed materials, audiovisuals, and educational programs for school personnel and children and also a list of organizations for further information. Other materials, including a comic book, posters, and training film, are available. References.

93.  Jesse, Rosalie C. **Children in Recovery.** New York: W.W. Norton and Co., 1989. 276 pp.

Focuses on the problems that children in middle childhood (ages 7-11) may experience during a parent's recovery from alcoholism or other drug abuse. Explores the dynamics of the addictive family system and the negative consequences for childhood development as well as parent-child and sibling relationships. Offers a family treatment model that involves the recovering parent as a co-therapist to help build a healthy parent-child relationship and to assist the child in developing a positive sense of self. Written as a guide for family therapists who deal with addicted families. References, index.

94.  Jorgensen, Donald G., Jr., and June A. Jorgensen. **Secrets Told by Children of Alcoholics: What Concerned Adults Need to Know.** Blue Ridge Summit, PA: TAB Books, 1990. 176 pp.

Records the personal stories of children aged 8-17 who come from families with an alcoholic parent. Describes their fears of abandonment and physical violence as well as their secret feelings of loneliness, anger, guilt, and embarrassment. Also discusses the processes of family intervention and recovery and their effects on COAs.

Written for therapists, educators, and concerned parents.
The appendixes include a list of resource organizations that
provide information or services for COAs or adult family
members.

95.     Lawson, Gary, James S. Peterson, and Ann Lawson.
        **Alcoholism and the Family: A Guide to Treatment
        and Prevention.** Rockville, MD: Aspen Publishers,
        1983. 296 pp.

        Provides theoretical and practical information for
therapists dealing with alcoholic families. Discusses the
most common theories regarding the development of
alcoholism and describes several different treatment
approaches (Alcoholics Anonymous, transactional analysis
and behavioral models). The bulk of the text focuses on
treatment issues related to the alcoholic family, including
family violence, sexual problems, and marital therapy. There
is a separate chapter dealing with children of alcoholics
that focuses on their problems, behaviors, and family roles,
with descriptions of several treatment programs geared
specifically to their needs. The final two chapters focus on
ways of preventing the development of alcohol problems in
other family members, particularly the children. Well
written and documented. References and index.

96.     Lerner, Rokelle, and Naiditch, Barbara. **Children Are
        People: Early Education in Chemical Abuse
        Prevention.** 2 vols. Revised and edited by Linda
        Christensen. St. Paul, MN: Children Are People,
        1986. varying pages.

        Presents an alcohol and drug education/prevention
curriculum for use with grades kindergarten-six. The
lessons are designed to be incorporated into health,
science, or social studies classes. For grades kindergarten-
three there are twenty lesson plans for each, with the
focus on exploring feelings, understanding families, making
decisions, and friendships. Beginning with grade four there

are thirty lessons, including information about alcohol and drugs, chemical dependency in the family, and coping with family problems. For each grade module there are suggested reading lists for children and for parents and teachers that include materials about young and adult children of alcoholics. There are also lists of audiovisual materials and resource organizations. Bibliography, illustrations.

97. Metzger, Lawrence. **From Denial to Recovery: Counseling Problem Drinkers, Alcoholics, and Their Families.** San Francisco: Jossey-Bass, 1988. 307 pp.

Provides counselors with helpful guidelines to identify and assess the extent of an individual's alcohol problem. Deals with the breakdown of denial and the designing of a treatment plan tailored to the alcoholic and the family. Includes a chapter that focuses specifically on children of alcoholics, covering their developmental needs from infancy through adulthood. Examines the roles that children assume within the alcoholic family and discusses treatment approaches, including school-based prevention programs and group therapy, for helping children cope successfully with the effects of an unhealthy family situation. There is also a brief section outlining the stages of recovery that are particularly important for adult children of alcoholics. A separate chapter addresses the process of dealing with the family (as a unit and as individuals) in a therapeutic setting in order to facilitate the recovery process for the alcoholic as well as the family members. Could be useful for spouses and ACOAs who want to understand more about the effects of alcoholism and the recovery process on the family. References and index.

98. Mills, Dixie, Charles Deutsch, and Lena DiCicco. **Decisions About Drinking: A Sequential Alcohol Education Curriculum for Grades 3-12.** 3d ed. Somerville, MA: CASPAR Alcohol Education Program, 1987. varying pages.

Nationally recognized curriculum based on a philosophy of providing knowledge and exploring student attitudes and values toward alcohol in order to help students make responsible decisions regarding their own alcohol use. The curriculum is divided into three modules-- elementary (grades 3-6), junior high (grades 7-9), and senior high (grades 10-12)--with 5-10 teaching units (4-7 in the elementary module) in each. The activities in each module cover basic information about alcohol, attitudes toward alcohol and drinking, responsible decision-making, and alcoholism and its effects on the family. It is recommended that the sessions on alcoholism be held at the end of the units so that children may be more comfortable in their discussions and teachers may have a chance to identify those children who are exhibiting signs of alcohol-related family problems. The outline for each unit includes objectives, description of activities, and materials needed, and master copies of handouts are also included. The introduction includes lists of resource materials, a glossary of terms, background information for teachers about alcohol and its use, and discussions of teaching techniques such as role play and group discussion. In addition there is a section on helping children from alcoholic families that discusses the teacher's role as helper and describes behaviors and attitudes that may identify COAs in the classroom. CASPAR offers inservice training to help school personnel implement this program in their schools. A primary module for grades K-3 is also available (see item 84). Bibliography.

99.    Moe, Jerry, and Don Pohlman. **Kid's Power: Healing Games for Children of Alcoholics.** Deerfield Beach, FL: Health Communications, 1989. 89 pp.

Describes twenty-six games designed to help young children of alcoholics (ages four to adolescence) explore their feelings and improve their coping skills for living with an alcoholic parent. The games are grouped into six areas of focus: feelings, chemical dependency, family, defenses, problem solving, and self-esteem. For each game there is a suggested age level, a description of the activity and its goals, a list of materials needed, and an example of someone playing the game. Most games are very simple in content and require few materials. The activities range from puppet shows to crossword puzzles. The authors do not advise using these games with children unless additional training and education on COA issues are obtained. Appendixes contain lists of films and national organizations for and about COAs. Bibliography.

100.    Molchan, Deborah S. **Our Secret Feelings: Activities for Children of Alcoholics in Support Groups.** Holmes Beach, FL: Learning Publications, 1989. 53 pp.

Describes activities for use by counselors and other professionals who work with children of alcoholics. Activities are designed for use with children aged 6-12; most are intended for use with COA support groups, but several are also appropriate in family therapy or individual sessions. Twelve exercises are outlined; each entry includes objective, setting (support group, family therapy, etc.), materials needed, and a brief description of the activity. The exercises cover such topics as expressing feelings, describing family experiences, understanding healthy relationships, and building self-esteem. The appendixes include supplementary materials such as sample worksheets. This text should only be used by those who have some knowledge of COA issues. References.

101.    Morehouse, Ellen R., and Claire M. Scola. **Children of Alcoholics: Meeting the Needs of the Young COA in the School Setting.** South Laguna, CA: National Association for Children of Alcoholics, 1986. 30 pp.

Presents information for teachers, school counselors, and related personnel about identifying and helping children of alcoholics. Describes the effects of parental alcoholism on children and offers suggestions to help educators recognize the common characteristics of COAs. Includes guidelines for counseling children in the schools and referring to outside resources. There are also helpful lists of teacher's guides as well as books, pamphlets, and audiovisual materials to be used with COAs.

102. National Institute on Alcohol Abuse and Alcoholism. **A Growing Concern: How to Provide Services for Children from Alcoholic Families.** Prepared by Barbara J. Waite and Meredith J. Ludwig. Washington, DC: U.S. Government Printing Office, 1983. 52 pp.

Identifies problems and needs experienced by children of alcoholics and explores a variety of approaches and caregivers to serve this population. Also examines special needs and services for ethnic and cultural groups (Blacks, Hispanics, Native Americans). Includes a reading list and descriptions of several programs in schools, communities, and treatment settings that deal with children of alcoholics. References, bibliography.

103. National Institute on Alcohol Abuse and Alcoholism. **Services for Children of Alcoholics.** NIAAA Research Monograph, No. 4. Washington, DC: U.S. Government Printing Office, 1981. 191 pp.

Proceedings of a seminar sponsored by the National Institute on Alcohol Abuse and Alcoholism in 1979 to examine program and policy issues for providing services to children of alcoholics. The conference focused on four major areas of service delivery: identification, intervention, treatment, and prevention. The monograph includes a summary of the discussion of each major topic area as well as copies of the discussion leaders' presentations and detailed descriptions of eight programs providing a wide range of services for COAs. References.

104.    Office for Substance Abuse Prevention. **Children of Alcoholics.** Kits 1-4. Rockville, MD: National Clearinghouse for Alcohol and Drug Information, 1988. varying pages.

Offers four kits with basic information on alcoholism and the special needs of children living with alcoholic parents. The kits are designed for the following audiences: kids (pre-teens and early teens), parents, therapists, and helpers (educators, community leaders, school nurses, etc.). Each provides suggestions for getting help or providing services for COAs. The adult kits also include annotated lists of published materials and resource organizations.

105.    Pickens, Roy W. **Children of Alcoholics.** Center City, MN: Hazelden, 1984. 25 pp.

Identifies four disorders that may be found in children of alcoholics and describes the symptoms and possible treatment or prevention for each: fetal alcohol syndrome, hyperactive child syndrome, adult alcoholism, and adult depression. References.

106.    Portney, Susan. **PICADA Students Concerned: A Support Group Curriculum.** Madison, WI: PICADA, 1988. 75 pp.

Presents twenty-four activities to be used with support groups for students who are concerned about or are affected by someone else's alcohol or other drug use. The curriculum is designed for use outside the classroom setting with facilitators who have some knowledge or training on substance abuse issues. Each activity includes objectives, materials needed, and step-by-step guidelines for how the activity is to be used. Sample copies of informational handouts are also included. The activities focus on group dynamics, the effects of alcohol and drug use on families, self-awareness, and coping skills. Includes a pre-group interview form to screen students for participation in groups. May be used with students from middle schools, junior or senior high schools.

107.    Robinson, Bryan E. **Working with Children of Alcoholics: The Practitioner's Handbook.** Lexington, MA: Lexington Books, 1989. 253 pp.

Presents guidelines to help a variety of practitioners--including teachers, counselors, social service and health care professionals--identify and help children living in alcoholic homes. Describes the survival roles that children adopt to cope with the alcoholic family situation and identifies the psychological, physical, academic, and behavioral problems that may be manifested by COAs. Offers recommendations for developing and evaluating programs for COAs and discusses several treatment strategies that have proved effective with this population. Also includes a review of the state of knowledge on the genetic and environmental factors in family alcohol abuse. The text is thoroughly documented from the research and professional literature on COAs. There is a very helpful annotated bibliography of books for and about COAs and ACOAs as well as descriptive lists of periodicals, audiovisuals, curriculum materials, therapeutic games, and resource organizations. References, bibliography, index.

108.    Stimpson, Helga, Jania R. Garcia, and Launa C. Lackey. **Children of Alcoholics: A Handbook for Teachers.** Sitka, AK: Sitka Council on Alcoholism and Other Drug Abuse, 1986. 44 pp.

Designed to improve awareness among elementary and secondary school teachers about the problems suffered by children of alcoholic parents and how they can be addressed in the school setting. Originally prepared for Montana schools, it has been revised with special material incorporated for Alaska teachers. The content covers the stages of alcoholism, the family roles and coping skills developed by COAs, guidelines for identifying COAs in the classroom, and specific suggestions to aid teachers in responding to the needs of affected children. There is a list of local and statewide resources for help for COAs in Alaska; however, the main content of the text could be applied in any school system. References and bibliography.

109.   Treadway, David C. **Before It's Too Late! Working with Substance Abuse in the Family.** New York: W.W. Norton and Co., 1989. 215 pp.

  Serves as a practical guidebook to help family therapists recognize and deal effectively with alcohol or other drug problems in families. Discusses the difficulty in identifying substance abuse problems when other family or individual issues are the presenting problems for treatment. Several chapters focus on couples therapy to deal with the substance abuse as well as other important issues such as trust and intimacy. There are two chapters specifically focusing on children of alcoholics. The first talks about working with children who are presented as the problem for therapy when, in fact, there is a problem with parental substance abuse. The second chapter offers a four-part treatment model to help adult children of alcoholics improve their own self-esteem and family relationships. This book provides much useful knowledge for family therapists who are not well trained in alcohol and drug problems. Bibliography, index.

110.   Typpo, Marion H., and Jill M. Hastings. **An Elephant in the Living Room.** 2 vols. Minneapolis: CompCare, 1984. 69 pp. (plus leader's guide, 124 pp.)

  Designed to help elementary school-aged children from families in which there is an alcohol or drug abusing member. The set includes a children's workbook with activities to help children understand and express their feelings, improve self-esteem and family relationships, and cope with problems caused by alcoholism or drug abuse. There is also a leader's guide for use by adult professionals, including counselors, teachers, and social workers. The guide contains information on the disease of alcoholism, family roles and models, child development (physical and social), and providing help in a variety of settings--schools, treatment centers, support groups--for children of alcoholics. Illustrations, references, bibliography.

111. Veenstra, Susan. **Children of Alcoholic Parents: A Handbook for Counselors and Teachers.** Cleveland Heights, Ohio: Alcoholism Services of Cleveland, 1987. 77 pp.

Offers guidelines to professionals who want to establish support groups for minor children of alcoholic parents. Describes the family roles and behavior patterns often assumed by COAs and suggests ways of identifying and recruiting children who might benefit from a group therapy setting. Discusses the mechanics of running a group, from selecting a co-facilitator to dealing with problem situations, and outlines the leader's responsibilities to group members, sponsoring agency, and families. There is a chapter on curriculum that describes activities on which to focus weekly sessions. This is followed by a chapter on processing that suggests ways of using weekly activities to identify and discuss negative emotions or behaviors. There are several short appendixes with helpful lists of films, readings, and curriculum materials for COAs, teachers, and therapists (some references, however, are incomplete). This handbook should be used only by counselors or teachers who have substantial background in alcohol-related issues. Bibliography.

112. Wright, Janet M. **Chemical Dependency and Violence: Working With Dually Affected Families. A Cross-Training Program Manual for Counselors and Advocates.** Madison: Wisconsin Clearinghouse, 1982. 134 pp.

Describes an innovative training course for counselors dealing with families in which there is alcohol or other drug abuse and domestic violence. The course is designed as a "cross-training" program in which staff from chemical dependency agencies will provide training on alcohol/drug abuse for staff from family violence agencies or shelters and vice versa. The text is divided into two main parts covering woman abuse and chemical dependency. The section on woman abuse contains nine sessions that deal with factors associated with woman abuse, intervention in abusing families, legal issues related to battering, and child abuse and incest. There are ten sessions on chemical dependency that focus on dependency as a family illness, assessment and intervention techniques, working with children of alcoholics, female chemical abuse, fetal alcohol syndrome, and group treatment for families with chemical abuse. The program format is extremely flexible; sessions may be combined or arranged in any manner or used independently as needed. Each session includes an outline of content and activities to be covered, discussion of major points, and references for any additional materials needed. The appendixes contain evaluation forms, a pre- and post-test on family violence, a list of recommended films, and handouts on woman abuse and on chemical dependency to be used with the training sessions.

## Journal Articles

113. Bogdaniak, Roman C., and Fred P. Piercy. "Therapeutic Issues of Adolescent Children of Alcoholics (AdCA) Groups." *International Journal of Group Psychotherapy* 37(1987): 569-88.

Describes a group therapy approach for adolescent children of alcoholics based on education about substance abuse, motivation to seek help for individual substance abuse problems, and development of appropriate coping skills. Presents a detailed description of the group process, including the setting and the major therapeutic issues (e.g., denial, guilt, separation, control, personal identity, and other family abuse). References.

114.    Brown, Sandra A., and Vicki A. Creamer. "Implications for Intervention of Family History of Alcohol Abuse." *Alcohol Health and Research World* 12(1987/88): 120-25.

Reviews the research literature on cross-generational alcohol abuse and applies this knowledge to the treatment of alcoholics and their families. Discusses the importance of determining family history of alcoholism in order to better understand and effectively treat alcoholics. Also emphasizes the importance of family environment during treatment and the need to alter dysfunctional family interactions to reduce the risk of future alcohol problems for offspring. References.

115.    DiLorenzo, Paul. "Children in Alcoholic Families: Risks of Abuse and Unwise Parenting." *Focus on Chemically Dependent Families* 10(Sept.-Oct. 1987): 18-19.

Discusses the difference between unwise and unsafe or abusive parenting practices in alcoholic families and the effects on children. Outlines several guidelines to follow when evaluating whether a child should be removed from an alcoholic home.

116.    Efron, Don, and Kip Veenendaal. "Videotaping in Groups for Children of Substance Abusers: A Strategy for Emotionally Disturbed, Acting Out Children." *Alcoholism Treatment Quarterly* 4(Summer 1987): 71-85.

Describes the use of videotaping as a therapeutic tool in groups with young children of alcoholics. Demonstrates how this technique of producing videos has proved successful with the more emotionally disturbed, disruptive group members by allowing them an acceptable medium for acting out feelings and anxieties. Presents vignettes of several videos and discusses how videotaping can be used to provide support for children in shame-based families. Bibliography.

117.    Feder, Susannah R. "Chemically Dependent Teenage Children of Alcoholics: A Closer Look at the Assumptions of Adolescent Treatment." *Focus on Family and Chemical Dependency* 9(May-June 1986): 14-15, 17-19.

Examines some treatment techniques commonly used with chemically dependent adolescents and discusses why these strategies may be ineffective with patients who come from alcoholic homes. Suggests a model of treatment for chemically dependent COAs that is based more on a teaching/training perspective rather than a confrontational/emotional nature. Emphasizes the need to help COAs learn how to care for themselves, how to clarify their values, and how to develop appropriate defenses and problem-solving skills.

118.    Gress, James R. "Alcoholism's Hidden Curriculum." *Student Assistance Journal* 1(Nov.-Dec. 1988): 45-46, 61.

Describes some of the problems and behaviors that children of alcoholics may exhibit in the classroom and outlines several suggestions for school personnel to provide information, materials, and programs to help. References.

119.    Hanson, Gloria, and Greg Liber. "A Model for the Treatment of Adolescent Children of Alcoholics." *Alcoholism Treatment Quarterly* 6, no. 2(1989): 53-69.

Identifies the developmental needs of adolescents and discusses how these may be interrupted by parental alcoholism. Describes a group therapy model for treatment of adolescent children of alcoholics that focuses on establishing a safe environment in which children can learn about family alcoholism and can begin to express their feelings and needs regarding the family situation. The group process also includes guidance for developing positive life skills. Bibliography.

120.    Hassett, Don G. "Family Alcoholism and Child Abuse--Where Do You Start?" *Focus on Family and Chemical Dependency* 8(July-Aug. 1985): 14-15, 31.

Discusses the incidence of child abuse and neglect among alcoholic families and the need for treatment strategies that encompass both problems. Advocates the incorporation of self-help programs such as Parents Anonymous and Alcoholics Anonymous into the treatment framework because they involve both parent and child. Identifies similarities of alcoholic and child abusing families and cites the need for better communication and cross-training between alcoholism therapists and child abuse workers.

121.    James, Mark R. "Listen to My Song: Music Therapy for COAs." *Alcoholism and Addiction* 8(Nov.-Dec. 1987): 22.

Describes music therapy as a useful tool in groups for children of alcoholics. Music can be used to encourage nonverbal expression of feelings, to increase cooperation among group members, and to develop a sense of group identity and trust among group members. This type of therapy is described as particularly appropriate with adolescents and young adults, for whom music is very important.

122.    Jesse, Rosalie C. "The Child in Recovery: Phase I--Disavowal." *Alcoholism and Addiction* 8(Nov.-Dec. 1987): 19.

Discusses the problems that children encounter during the initial phase of their alcoholic parent's recovery. The author defines children's reactions to parental alcoholism as disavowal--a protective mechanism that shields children from truly comprehending the family situation--rather than a denial of that situation. She recommends that the initial phase of therapy for children focus not on the family situation or potential relapse but on activities designed to promote emotional support, self-soothing, and the development of a bond with a trusted adult (therapist) who can facilitate expression of needs.

123.   Jones, John W. "The Children of Alcoholics Screening Test: A Validity Study." *Bulletin of the Society of Psychologists in Addictive Behaviors* 2(1983): 155-63.

Establishes the reliability and validity of the Children of Alcoholics Screening Test (CAST) and describes how it is used to identify COAs. Also demonstrates how it can be used to diagnose parental alcoholism and to strengthen treatment by breaking through denial. References.

124.   Koll, L.T. 'Scotte.' "Meeting Special Needs: A Holistic Approach to Chemical Abuse." *Student Assistance Journal* 1(Nov.-Dec. 1988): 25-29.

Describes the development and results of a pilot student assistance program to meet the needs of youth at high risk for alcohol and drug problems. Three groups--children of alcoholics, children abusing alcohol or other drugs, and children doing poorly in school--were targeted for service through education and support groups. The groups focused on improving life skills, building self-esteem, developing coping skills and personal values, learning to handle feelings and to relate to others, and acquiring communication skills.

125.    Krebsbach, Sara. "How Teachers Can Help Children of Alcoholics." *Student Assistance Journal* 1(Jan.-Feb. 1989): 23-26.

Offers practical advice for teachers to identify and help children of alcoholics in the classroom. Describes a hierarchical model of listening intensities to help teachers encourage troubled students to talk about their problems.

126.    Lackey, Launa. "Children from Alcoholic Families: Impact and Identification in the Classroom." *Focus on Chemically Dependent Families* 10(Mar.-Apr. 1987): 27-28.

Discusses the importance of including drug and alcohol information in the classroom as a means of preventing future substance abuse problems, especially among high-risk children of alcoholic families. Focuses on the role of alcohol/drug professionals and provides practical suggestions to help them cooperate with school personnel in providing alcohol and drug programs, including curricula, classroom presentations, and in-service teacher training.

127.    Lerner, Rokelle. "Children in Family Treatment--Are They Still Forgotten?" *Focus on Family and Chemical Dependency* 9(May-June 1986): 6-7, 45.

Advocates the inclusion of pre-adolescent children in parental or family recovery programs. Discusses the importance of recognizing and treating the problems that young children may have developed from living in an alcoholic home as well as the need to include parenting skills in family recovery programs. Also describes some of the cues that can help teachers and counselors identify COAs and get help for them even when the parents are not in recovery.

128.    Liles, Ray E., and Diane Childs. "Similarities in
        Family Dynamics of Incest and Alcohol Abuse: Issues
        for Clinicians." *Alcohol Health and Research World*
        11(Fall 1986): 66-69.

Discusses the similar etiologies of alcoholism and
incest as well as their frequent interrelationship. Describes
the roles played by the offending parent, the spouse, and
the child victim and outlines the major issues that must be
dealt with in therapy for all family members. References.

129.    Macdonald, Donald I., and Sheila B. Blume. "Children
        of Alcoholics." *American Journal of Diseases of
        Children* 140(1988): 750-54.

Provides an overview of the prevalence of family
alcohol problems and their effects on children. Identifies
several reasons for the underdiagnosis of alcoholism and
discusses the role of the pediatrician in diagnosis and
referral. Recommends that pediatricians serve as advocates
to obtain more and better services for children and
families with chemical dependency. References.

130.    McElligatt, Kate. "Identifying and Treating Children
        of Alcoholic Parents." *Social Work Education*
        9(1986): 55-70.

Describes the physical, emotional, and behavioral
problems from which children of alcoholics often suffer and
discusses how these may be identified in the school
setting. Provides an overview of the effects of parental
alcoholism on children, focusing on the roles that children
may adopt in order to cope. Points out the importance of
teachers, guidance counselors, and school social workers
in helping COAs through classroom instruction, support
groups, and individual counseling. Cites the CASPAR
curriculum **Decisions About Drinking** (see item 98) as an
example of an effective education/prevention program.
References.

131.    Manning, D. Thompson. "Books as Therapy for Children of Alcoholics." *Child Welfare* 66(1987): 35-43.

Discusses the therapeutic value of books as a tool for helping young and adolescent children of alcoholics understand and cope with parental alcoholism. Describes the stages of "bibliotherapy" and demonstrates how this process may be used to break through a COA's denial in a nonthreatening manner. Identifies three types of literature that may be used with COAs--fictional accounts of COA experiences, nonfiction books about alcohol and its effects on the family, and books for professionals to help them identify and deal with COA issues--and offers examples of each type. Also includes guidelines for selecting literature and for determining readability for age groups. References.

132.    Moses, Debra. "For Kids Only--A Child's Concept of Alcoholism." *Focus on Family and Chemical Dependency* 9(Nov.-Dec. 1986): 28-29.

Describes the program at Livengrin Foundation in Pennsylvania designed to help children of alcoholics aged 7-12 years old. The program uses art therapy, play, storytelling, and group discussion to help children get in touch with their confusion and their feelings. Includes a "feelings chart" for counselors, educators, and social service workers that outlines the needs of children as well as the symptoms of alcoholism and codependency.

133.    Naiditch, Barbara. "Rekindled Spirit of a Child: Intervention Strategies for Shame with Elementary Age Children of Alcoholics." *Alcoholism Treatment Quarterly* 4(Summer 1987): 57-69.

Outlines the developmental stages of childhood and demonstrates how shame occurs and is reinforced for children born into alcoholic families. Suggests four intervention techniques that may be used to relieve shame for elementary school-aged COAs: support groups, play, affirmations, and a Twelve Step program. Useful for school counselors and other therapists who work with children. References.

134. Oliver-Diaz, Philip. "How to Help Recovering Families Struggle to Get Well: What Treatment Centers Need to Know About Helping Children of Alcoholics." *Focus on Chemically Dependent Families* 11(April-May 1988): 20-21, 49-50.

Offers practical advice to help treatment personnel deal more effectively with children of alcoholics. Discusses how children may react to their parents in recovery and demonstrates why they may feel confused, left out, or embarrassed by their parents' behavior. Provides guidance to help treatment personnel know when and how to explain the recovery process to children and advocates the use of support groups only when a child feels ready.

135. Pilat, Joanne M., and John W. Jones. "Identification of Children of Alcoholics: Two Empirical Studies." *Alcohol Health and Research World* 9(Winter 1984/85): 27-33, 36.

Discusses the use of the Children of Alcoholics Screening Test (CAST) as a tool to identify children who are living or have lived with an alcoholic parent. The CAST measures children's feelings, attitudes, perceptions, and experiences related to their parents' drinking, and it can be used with young children as well as adult children of alcoholics. Establishes reliability and validity of the CAST and describes its applications in two research projects, which focused on identification of COAs in a high school classroom setting and prevalence of parental alcoholism in families of helping professionals. Also discusses treatment needs of COAs and use of the CAST in detection and prevention of problems. Includes a copy of the instrument. References.

136.  Riddell, Alice M. "'I Never Knew There Were So Many of Us': A Model Early Intervention Alcohol Program." *Alcohol Health and Research World* 12(Winter 1987/88): 110-13, 124.

Describes a program developed by a school district in Queens, New York City, to identify children of alcoholics and provide counseling and group support within the school setting for their problems. The program provides basic information on alcohol and alcohol-related problems, including family alcoholism, to fifth and sixth grade students as well as teachers and parents. Students who are identified by the program staff as possible COAs are channelled into support groups to reduce isolation and shame and to build self-esteem. In addition, students may be given individual counseling or may be referred to family counseling. Recommendations for expanding or replicating this program are provided.

137.  Saulnier, Christine. "Intervention with Visually Impaired Children of Alcoholics." *Alcohol Health and Research World* 13, no. 2(1989): 133-37.

Identifies some of the special problems that may be experienced by visually impaired children or adults from homes with an alcoholic parent. Discusses why these problems may not be readily apparent to social service workers or special education personnel and offers suggestions for recognizing and dealing with these alcohol-related issues. References.

138.  Starr, Ann Marie C. "Recovery for the Alcoholic Family: Family Systems Treatment Model." *Social Casework* 70(1989): 348-54.

Outlines a three-stage model for treating alcoholic families. Identifies the stages of family development and describes how individual members and the family as a whole are affected by alcoholism in each of the stages.

Discusses some of the specific problems that children may encounter and suggests tasks to help children and parents reorient their behavior and restructure family relationships during recovery from alcoholism.

139. Tharinger, Deborah J., and Margaret E. Koranek. "Children of Alcoholics--At Risk and Unserved: A Review of Research and Service Roles for School Psychologists." *School Psychology Review* 17(1988): 166-91.

Discusses the potential role of school psychologists in identifying and helping children of alcoholics. Reviews the research literature on the effects of alcoholism on the family and on childhood development and explores such issues as whether COAs are more at risk to develop behavioral, emotional, or social problems than children of nonalcoholics. Identifies the major obstacles for school psychologists to overcome in dealing with this population and suggests ways to help, such as advocacy, identification, assessment, intervention, and prevention activities. References.

See also: 5, 9, 11, 13, 30, 34, 42, 74, 78, 146-47, 151, 162, 164, 232, 235, 246, 249-50.

## 5. RECOVERY

### Books and Pamphlets

The literature in this chapter is designed to help children or other family members deal with the effects of family alcoholism on their personal lives. Materials offer guidelines for handling emotions, developing effective coping skills, and seeking further help. Items for use primarily by therapists or other professionals are covered in chapter 4, **Children: Treatment.**

140. Al-Anon Family Groups. **Alateen--Hope for Children of Alcoholics.** New York: Al-Anon Family Group Headquarters, 1973. 115 pp.

Explains the philosophy and workings of the Alateen program, designed to help teenagers cope with an alcoholic in the family. Describes the basic elements of Alateen, including the Twelve Steps, Twelve Traditions, and Slogans, and offers personal stories of teenagers who have been in the program. Also provides general information on alcoholism as well as specific information on organizing Alateen groups and planning meetings.

141. Al-Anon Family Groups. **Facts About Alateen.** New York: Al-Anon Family Group Headquarters, 1969. 2 pp.

Outlines the basic purposes and structure of the Alateen support groups for teenagers who have alcoholism in their families (or among their close friends).

142.     Al-Anon Family Groups. **If Your Parents Drink Too Much**.... New York: Al-Anon Family Group Headquarters, 1974. 24 pp.

Depicts the problems of three teenagers who have alcoholic parents. Briefly describes the Alateen program and shows how two of the troubled teens find help for their family problems through Alateen.

143.     Al-Anon Family Groups. **What's "Drunk," Mama?** New York: Al-Anon Family Group Headquarters, 1977. 30 pp.

Presents basic information on alcoholism for young children who have a parent with a drinking problem. Sensitively describes the reasons for the behaviors of the alcoholic and the nonalcoholic parent and also discusses the child's own emotional reactions. Explains briefly about the Al-Anon and Alateen programs that can help families cope with an alcoholic. Illustrations.

144.     Al-Anon Family Groups. **Youth and the Alcoholic Parent.** New York: Al-Anon Family Group Headquarters, 1979. 12 pp.

Briefly describes the background and purpose of Alateen--a fellowship of children (aged 12-20) from alcoholic families. Includes answers to frequently asked questions about parental alcoholic behavior and offers suggestions for coping with family problems caused by alcohol abuse.

145.     Balcerzak, Ann M. **Hope for Young People with Alcoholic Parents.** Center City, MN: Hazelden, 1981. 13 pp.

Written for elementary and junior high school-aged children who have an alcoholic parent. Describes alcoholism as a disease and explains why alcoholics continue to drink and how alcohol affects their behavior. Offers practical suggestions for coping with such alcohol-related problems as violence, broken promises, and embarrassing parental behavior. Also suggests further sources for help such as other family members, teachers and guidance counselors, clergy, and the Alateen program for teenage children of alcoholics.

146.    Black, Claudia. **My Dad Loves Me, My Dad Has a Disease**. Denver: MAC Publishing, 1982. 84 pp.

Combines illustrations with easy-to-read explanations for young children (through elementary school) with alcoholic parents. The book describes symptoms of alcoholic behavior, such as blackouts and inconsistent behavior, and helps children to examine their feelings about an alcoholic parent. There is also a section designed to help children cope with parental recovery. All illustrations are drawn by children, and blank pages are included for young readers to add their own contributions. May be used in conjunction with children's therapy groups or individual counseling.

147.    Daley, Dennis C. **Family Recovery Workbook for Families Affected by Chemical Dependency**. Bradenton, FL: Human Services Institute, 1987. 23 pp. + appendixes.

Directed primarily at spouses or partners of alcoholics to help them understand and cope with the effects of alcoholism on the family. Uses inventories (or checklists) of the behavioral, psychological, physical, and social effects of alcohol and drug use to determine the seriousness of the alcoholic's problem as well as the extent to which the spouse and children have been affected. Also offers brief but practical suggestions for engaging in family recovery and avoiding or dealing with relapse of the alcoholic or other family members. The chapter on helping the children in an alcoholic family focuses on identifying negative behaviors and attitudes as well as health problems that may be related to the family environment and suggests involving the children in counseling or self-help programs such as Alateen. Recommended for use by families in conjunction with individual, group, or family therapy. There is a brief resource list of organizations in the appendix, but several of the addresses are out of date. Bibliography.

148.     Daley, Dennis C. **Surviving Addiction: A Guide for Alcoholics, Drug Addicts, and Their Families.** New York: Gardner Press, 1988. 251 pp.

Provides basic information about alcoholism and other drug addiction and the effects on individuals and family members. Part one describes the process of addiction, while part two focuses on the physical, psychological, and social effects on the alcoholic or drug addict. There is also information on recovery, relapse, and sources of help for alcoholics. Part three deals with the problems of family members, including a separate chapter on children of alcoholics covering physical health, emotional, and social problems. Provides guidelines for family recovery and preventing relapse of destructive codependent behaviors. Also presents information on types of treatment and self-help programs for children, adult children, and parents. Bibliography, index.

149.     Hornik-Beer, Edith L. **A Teenager's Guide to Living with an Alcoholic Parent.** Center City, MN: Hazelden, 1984. 83 pp.

Answers questions from teenage children of alcoholics about their parents' alcoholic behaviors and their own related feelings and experiences. Covers such topics as bringing friends home, sharing family responsibilities, getting help to cope with parental alcoholism, and what to expect from a newly-sober parent.

150.  **How You Can Help**. New York: Children of Alcoholics Foundation, 1986. 1 pp.

Outlines steps that parents, teachers, or other adults can take to help children or adults who have an alcoholic parent. Presents a brief summary of the types of problems that children and adults may suffer as a result of coping with parental alcoholism. Provides separate lists of suggestions for helping these children and adults, including involvement in school or after-work activities and identifying possible sources of help. The text presumes the reader has some understanding of alcoholism as a family disease.

151.  Ketcham, Katherine, and Ginny L. Gustafson. **Living on the Edge: A Guide to Intervention for Families with Drug and Alcohol Problems**. New York: Bantam Books, 1989. 259 pp.

Describes the process of intervention, by which families of alcohol or drug abusers can coordinate their concern about the addiction and help motivate the abuser into treatment. Discusses the stages of addiction and identifies warning signs. Offers numerous case examples of families who recognized the problem and participated in the intervention process. Also offers helpful suggestions for choosing a counselor and preparing for an intervention. The family situations described deal with the concerns and needs of children, adult children, and spouses of alcoholics and drug abusers. The text is appropriate for older teenagers as well as adults or family counselors. An appendix provides basic facts about several commonly abused drugs, including alcohol. There is also a resource list of organizations for help or further information. Bibliography, index.

152.    Leite,  Evelyn.  **Mending  Family  Relationships.**
        Minneapolis: Community Intervention, 1987. 35 pp.

        Examines,  from  a  recovering  parent's  point  of  view,
the  problems  frequently  suffered  by  children  in  alcoholic
families.  Offers  practical  suggestions  to  help  parents
establish  healthy  family  relationships  and  to  avoid  passing
on  to  their  children  dysfunctional  behaviors  such  as  shame,
guilt,  fear,  abuse  and  neglect,  or  chemical  dependence.

153.    Porterfield, Kay M. **Familiar Strangers.** Center City,
        MN: Hazelden, 1984. 145 pp.

        Offers  practical  advice  to  help  recovering  alcoholic
or  drug-addicted  parents  rebuild  positive  relationships  with
their  children.  Describes  some  of  the  ways  children  learn
to  cope  with  their  parents'  addiction  and  suggests  ways  for
parents  to  encourage  new  family  behaviors  based  on
communication  and  trust.  Includes  a  chapter  on  how  to  talk
to  children  about  alcohol  and  drug  use.

154.    Seixas,  Judith  S.  **What  Can  You  Do  To  Help  a**
        **Friend?**  New  York:  Children  of  Alcoholics
        Foundation, n.d. 1 pp.

        Offers  advice  to  children  who  want  to  help  a  friend
that  is  living  in  an  alcoholic  home.  Includes  suggestions  to
encourage  the  friend  to  participate  in  after-school
activities  and  to  seek  out  teachers  or  counselors  who  may
be  able  to  help.  The  text  presumes  that  the  reader  has
some  understanding  of  alcoholism  as  a  family  disease.
Appropriate  for  upper-elementary  through  junior  high
school ages.

155.    Sinberg, Janet, and Dennis Daley. **I Can Talk About**
        **What  Hurts:  A  Book  for  Kids  in  Homes  Where**
        **There's  Chemical  Dependency.**  Illustrated  by  Tim
        Hartman. Center City, MN: Hazelden, 1989. 48 pp.

Written for kids aged 8-12 to explain the disease of chemical dependency and how it affects parents and children. Provides basic information about alcoholism and other drug abuse and recounts brief experiences of children who have lived with an alcoholic or addicted parent. Describes the process of recovery for the alcoholic and for family members and urges children to talk about their problems to parents, counselors, or members of support groups such as Alateen or Alatot. Includes guidelines to help parents open communication with children on alcohol and drug problems. Glossary, bibliography.

## Journal Articles

156.     Robinson, Bryan E. "Wearing Mommy's Apron, Filling Daddy's Shoes: COAs--Latchkey Children by Default." *Focus on Chemically Dependent Families* 11(June-July 1988): 22-23, 39-40.

Describes the similarities between latchkey children, who are without supervision until a working parent gets home, and children of alcoholics, who come home to a nonfunctional alcoholic parent. Offers an instrument--the Latchkey Risk Quotient for Children of Alcoholics--to help determine the level of risk for COAs who are nonsupervised (or poorly supervised). Provides practical suggestions to help sober parents minimize risk and enhance self-care skills for COAs.

See also: 46, 51, 67, 72, 81, 85, 93, 138, 162, 285, 310.

## 6. FICTION

### Books and Pamphlets

This chapter describes novels and other fictional accounts about living with an alcoholic parent. Includes some material appropriate for the entire family as well as items written for young adult and elementary school-aged audiences.

157.   Brooks, Bruce. **No Kidding.** New York: Harper and
       Row, 1989. 207 pp.

Provides an interesting twist to the fictional story of a fourteen-year-old boy who assumes physical and emotional responsibility for his recovering alcoholic mother and his younger brother. The book is set in the twenty-first century United States when alcoholism has been legally declared an epidemic, and the treatment system has become federally subsidized and regulated. The author takes a cynical view of much of the rhetoric and treatment practices currently surrounding children of alcoholics. In this novel COAs have been officially designated "alcoholic offspring" (AOs), and they are identified and treated primarily through the schools' rigid doctrinaire programs. This book offers very thoughtful insight into where the current COA movement may be heading; however, the prose is generally stiff and presumes some background knowledge of COAs. It would not be appropriate for young teens.

158.    Crosbie, Karol. **Mom and Me.** Minneapolis: Community Intervention, 1989. 30 pp.

Tells the story of a seventh-grade boy who learns about his mother's alcoholism. Describes the boy's futile attempts to cheer up his family and his negative attention-getting behaviors in school, which finally bring him into contact with the school counselor. With the counselor's help, David and his family are able to better understand and cope with the mother's alcoholism. Appropriate for a pre-teen audience. Illustrations.

159.    DeClements, Barthe. No Place for Me. New York: Viking Penguin, 1987. 136 pp.

Sensitive portrayal of an adolescent girl's feelings of abandonment and isolation due to her mother's alcoholism. While her mother is in treatment and her stepfather is preoccupied with his business, Copper Jones is bounced from a series of relatives until she lands with her Aunt Maggie, whom everyone thinks is a witch. From this unorthodox role model Copper begins to learn more about herself and the possibilities life has to offer her. Written for young teens and pre-teens.

160.    Figueroa, Ronny. **Pablito's Secret (El Secreto de Pablito).** Deerfield Beach, FL: Health Communications, 1984. 30 pp.

Tells the story of a child who discloses to a friend the secret of his father's drinking problem and learns about the disease of alcoholism. Written in Spanish and English for elementary school-aged children. Illustrations.

161.    Fox, Paula. **The Moonlight Man.** New York: Bradbury Press, 1986. 179 pp.

Beautifully written account of a fifteen-year-old girl's summer visit with her alcoholic father. This is a sensitive yet realistic story of a daughter struggling to know her divorced father while also trying to understand his obsession with drinking and how it has affected his life. Among the many lessons she learns is that it is possible to love someone for himself and his dreams in spite of his addiction to alcohol. Especially recommended for teenagers.

162.    Hall, Lindsey, and Leigh Cohn. **Dear Kids of Alcoholics**. Carlsbad, CA: Gurze Books, 1988. 94 pp.

Candidly describes the experiences of living with an alcoholic parent, as told by a pre-teenage boy. Discusses the alcoholic parent's behavior as well as the emotional and behavioral reactions of the other family members. Also covers treatment and recovery, including a very good description of the guided intervention technique for motivating an alcoholic into treatment. The emphasis of the text is on alcoholism as a family disease that requires full family participation for effective recovery. Written for children ages 8-17; may also be used by educators, counselors, or parents working with COAs. Glossary, illustrations.

163.    Hamilton, Dorothy. **Mari's Mountain**. Scottdale, PA: Herald Press, 1978. 130 pp.

Recounts the various adventures of a teenage girl who leaves home to escape the physical abuse of her alcoholic mother. Describes her difficulties in finding work and a place to live and deals sensitively with her reunion with her mother and the beginning of their new life together. Suitable for upper-elementary or junior high school ages. Illustrations.

164.    Hyatt, Lillian L. **A Triangle of Ashes**. San Francisco: Lifeline Press, 1986. 94 pp.

Constructs a fictional case history of a family's struggle with the effects of parental alcoholism. The story

involves an alcoholic father, two children, and a
nonalcoholic stepmother who consults a family therapist in
order to prevent the complete destruction of her family.
Through successive therapy sessions, gradually involving all
family members, the issues of codependency, anger,
resentment, guilt, fear, family roles, and acting-out
behavior are discussed. After the father has completed a
treatment program, the changes in the family system are
explored. The book concludes with a clinical epilogue for
therapists that highlights the issues covered in the
chapters. This book is extremely readable and would be
useful in helping spouses as well as adolescent children of
alcoholics understand the distortion in their lives. It would
also be useful for therapists who work with alcoholic
families. Glossary, bibliography.

165.    Kenny, Kevin, and Helen Krull. **Sometimes My Mom
        Drinks Too Much.** Milwaukee: Raintree Childrens
        Books, 1980. 31 pp.

        Describes the difficulties a young girl experiences
as a result of her mother's drinking problem. Explains that
alcoholism is a disease that is no one's fault and suggests
persons (other family members, teachers) that may be able
to help a child understand and cope. Written for younger
elementary school-aged children. Illustrations.

166.    Oppenheimer, Joan L. **Francesca, Baby.** New York:
        Scholastic Book Services, 1976. 156 pp.

        Absorbing story of a teenage girl's difficulties in
coping with her alcoholic mother. Focuses on problems with
family and social relationships and incorporates helpful
information about Alateen, Al-Anon, and Alcoholics
Anonymous. Written for junior and senior high school ages.

167.    Robe, Lucy B. **Haunted Inheritance.** Minneapolis:
        CompCare, 1980. 160 pp.

Includes mystery, suspense, romance, and information about alcoholism within the tale of a young woman's unusual inheritance. Contains some discussion of the disease aspect of alcoholism and its effects on the family (including fetal alcohol syndrome). Interesting reading for teenagers.

168.    Scales, Cynthia G. **Potato Chips for Breakfast: An Autobiography.** Delaware Water Gap, PA: Quotidian, 1986. 167 pp.

Uses a diary format to tell the story of a teenager's unhappy experiences living in a home with two active alcoholic parents. The diary covers a period of three years until the author's first marriage. The entries describe graphically the inconsistent and often violent behaviors and the verbal abuse and neglect by the parents as well as the author's teenage responses (including delinquent behavior). The text is highly emotional but could be used to help teenaged or adult children of alcoholics learn to acknowledge their pain of growing up in an alcoholic home.

169.    Seabrooke, Brenda. **Home Is Where They Take You In.** New York: William Morrow and Co., 1980. 190 pp.

Chronicles the coming-of-age of a twelve-year-old girl with an alcoholic mother. Describes Benicia's loneliness and isolation, brought on by the behavior of her drunken mother and her mother's abusive boyfriend. Presents a sensitive portrayal of her friendship with a poor young man suffering from ringworm and describes the benefits they receive from their association with Jack and Andrea, who provide healthy role models and positive reinforcement for their self-esteem.

170.    Stanek, Muriel. **Don't Hurt Me, Mama.** Illustrated by
        Helen Cogancherry. Niles, IL: Albert Whitman and
        Co., 1983. 29 pp.

        Tells the story of a young girl whose mother
develops a drinking problem and becomes physically abusive
after her husband deserts the family. With the help of an
observant school nurse the abuse pattern is identified and
the mother is able to get help for her problems. The text
is simple and beautifully illustrated. It provides a clear
message of hope and understanding for young children in
abusive and alcoholic families. Appropriate for use with
younger elementary school-aged or preschool-aged children.
Illustrations.

        See also: 53-54, 87.

# PART TWO

# ADULT CHILDREN OF ALCOHOLICS

# INTRODUCTION

In recent years many adult children of alcoholics have sought treatment for emotional and interpersonal problems which they have attributed in some measure to growing up with an alcoholic parent. Several factors have contributed to this phenomenon: the growing body of clinical literature dealing with the consequences of being raised in an alcoholic home, empirical research studies documenting the effects of alcoholism on the family, and the rapidly increasing number of ACOA groups and self-help books aimed at this population (Vannicelli 1989). While many social service professionals have remained skeptical about the validity of the "adult child" concept, others have embraced it as symbolic of the loss of normal childhood development and the attempt to cope with the memory of the past as well as the present (Johnson and Bennett 1989). Vannicelli (1989) has demonstrated that this "adult child" concept, by relating current problems and methods of interaction and coping to earlier experiences with the family of origin, is well grounded in psychodynamic theory.

Much of the adult child literature has focused on identifying common characteristics of ACOAs and offering practical guidelines toward recovery from the effects of negative childhood experiences. This literature has emerged more recently than the literature on children of alcoholics as a whole; the first major work was Janet Woititz' **Adult Children of Alcoholics** published in 1983. Although the bulk of the material is still self-oriented, clinical findings and popular beliefs have generated an increasing number of empirical studies of problems and coping mechanisms of ACOAs. Many of the suppositions in the professional literature have not been documented by research, especially those dealing with feelings, which are particularly difficult to measure.

Another problem with the adult child literature is the looseness of the definition. The "adult child" concept is often applied to persons who were raised in other types of dysfunctional (problem) families. In fact, some of the literature never really discusses alcohol or other drug problems in the family but instead offers rather broad guidelines for developing healthier lifestyles. While this material may be appropriate and helpful to ACOAs, it lacks the value of addressing how and what specific adult problems may be attributed to growing up with parental substance abuse. Although addictions and compulsive behaviors may share some characteristics, research has shown that not all persons react in the same way to their effects. Many children of alcoholics have coped successfully with their alcoholic parents and have developed into well-adjusted adults.

Part two of this bibliography encompasses the research and professional literature on adult children of alcoholics as well as self-help materials designed to assist ACOAs in recovering from the negative effects of growing up in an alcoholic home. There are no general reference tools (bibliographies, directories) dealing exclusively with adult children, but the reference materials in chapter one all include adult populations.

## References

Johnson, Jeannette L., and Linda A. Bennett. **Adult Children of Alcoholics: Theory and Research.** New Brunswick, NJ: Rutgers Center of Alcohol Studies, 1989.

Vannicelli, Marsha. **Group Psychotherapy with Adult Children of Alcoholics: Treatment Tools and Countertransference Considerations.** New York: Guilford Press, 1989.

Woititz, Janet G. **Adult Children of Alcoholics.** Deerfield Beach, FL: Health Communications, 1983.

# 7. RESEARCH

## Books and Pamphlets

This chapter cites literature on research primarily dealing with adult children of alcoholics. For studies covering younger children as well as adult children, see chapter 2, **Children: Research**. For research material on treatment techniques and theory see also chapter 9, **Adult Children: Treatment**.

171.    Ackerman, Robert J. Same House, **Different Homes: Why Adult Children of Alcoholics Are Not All the Same**. Deerfield Beach, FL: Health Communications, 1987. 55 pp.

Presents the results and brief analysis of a study of 1,000 adults, half of whom had at least one alcoholic parent. The study was designed to assess personality characteristics of adult children of alcoholics as compared to adults of nonalcoholic parents. Findings demonstrate how ACOAs may have reacted differently to similar situations. There are also some interesting examinations of the influence of gender, age, positive offsetting factors, and cultural considerations on how children are affected by parental alcoholism. Tables, references.

172.    Johnson, Jeannette L., and Linda A. Bennett. **Adult Children of Alcoholics: Theory and Research.** New

Brunswick, NJ: Rutgers Center of Alcohol Studies, 1989. 19 pp.

Reviews the current state of research on issues related to adult children of alcoholics. Highlights four major areas of research on factors associated with ACOAs--transmission of alcoholism, family disruption, personality, and general studies of adaptation--and briefly discusses the major contributions in each area. Also discusses the current approaches of group therapy and family systems therapy for dealing with the problems of ACOAs and offers suggestions for future directions in research and treatment. Written for researchers, therapists, and ACOAs. Bibliography.

### Journal Articles

173.    Ackerman, Robert J. "Family Findings: Does Gender Make a Difference? New Research on Adult Children." *Focus on Chemically Dependent Families* 11(Feb.-Mar. 1988): 12-13.

Reports findings from the National Adult Children of Alcoholics Research Study, which rated ACOAs on twenty personality characteristics. Gender appeared to have a significant impact on issues related to adult children; however, the data did not reveal whether the gender of parent or child (or an interaction of both) had the most effect.

174.    Alterman, Arthur I., Robert Bridges, and Ralph E. Tarter. "Drinking Behavior of High Risk College Men: Contradictory Preliminary Findings." *Alcoholism: Clinical and Experimental Research* 10(1986): 305-10.

Discusses findings from a study that compared drinking behavior of high risk college males (sons of alcoholic or problem drinking fathers) with a low risk group of similar background from families without alcohol problems. Contrary to expectations, the low risk group was found to have a greater involvement with alcohol, including greater incidence of intoxication. In addition, sensation seeking, which has been correlated with frequency of drinking in other research, was found to be significantly greater in low risk subjects. The authors suggest that further research is needed on environmental and psychological influences on drinking behavior of high and low risk persons. References.

175. Beardslee, W.R., L. Son, and G.E. Vaillant. "Exposure to Parental Alcoholism During Childhood and Outcome in Adulthood: A Prospective Longitudinal Study." *British Journal of Psychiatry* 149(1986): 584-91.

Analyzes data from an existing prospective forty-year longitudinal study of working class families to determine effect of exposure to alcoholism in the childhood family environment and outcome during adulthood. Exposure to family alcoholism was found to be significantly related to development of alcohol abuse, time spent in jail, sociopathy, and death rates but not to overall adult psychological functioning, unemployment, or poor physical health. The findings also demonstrate the resiliency of children of alcoholics since the majority of exposed subjects that were evaluated functioned similarly to the non-exposed group despite the presence of severe alcoholism and family discord during childhood. References.

176. Beidler, Robert J. "Adult Children of Alcoholics: Is It Really a Separate Field for Study?" *Drugs and Society* 3, no. 3-4(1989): 133-41.

Outlines several core issues important in understanding the process of adjustment of adult children of alcoholics. Argues that "adult children" should not be used as a diagnostic label that assumes a set of problems or dysfunctional behaviors. The author suggests instead a phenomenological orientation that looks at parental alcoholism as only one factor in adjustment of adult offspring. Briefly reviews some of the major research on the effects of alcoholism on the family and on maladjustment among ACOAs. Also discusses general theory on ACOAs and on adult adjustment and demonstrates some of the discrepancies between theory and existing research. References.

177.    Bennett, Linda A., Steven J. Wolin, David Reiss, and Martha A. Teitelbaum. "Couples at Risk for Transmission of Alcoholism: Protective Influences." *Family Process* 26(1987): 111-29.

Describes a two-generation, sociocultural model of the transmission of alcoholism in families and identifies several factors which appear to be significantly related to the risk of developing alcoholism. The study focused on married children of alcoholics, their spouses, and the families of origin for all the subjects. Specific family rituals from the families of origin and from the current families of the adult children were examined to determine their relationship to development of alcoholism in the adult children. Findings showed that adult children whose family rituals were relatively undisrupted by a parent's alcoholism were less likely to develop alcohol problems of their own. Likewise, adult children whose spouses came from families with strong, positive family rituals were also less likely to suffer problems. Those adult children whose families of origin did not develop strong rituals or whose spouses came from alcoholic families were at much higher risk of becoming alcoholic. References.

178.    Berkowitz, Alan, and H. Wesley Perkins. "Personality Characteristics of Children of Alcoholics." *Journal of Consulting and Clinical Psychology* 56(1988): 206-9.

Discusses the results of a study to examine effects of family alcoholism on personality characteristics of first- and second-year college students. Children of alcoholics were identified from an initial alcohol survey; they were then tested along with their peers from nonalcoholic families on a variety of personality measures. Several aspects of personality functioning--including impulsiveness, lack of tension, directiveness, and sociability--appeared to be unaffected by the COA experience. However, certain effects varied according to the gender of the COA, and there was a significant difference in the effects of an alcoholic parent's gender on the self-depreciation of daughters. This study points to the resiliency of COAs as evidenced by adaptive functioning on a variety of personality measures while identifying potential negative effects that should be addressed by researchers and clinicians. References.

179.   Black, Claudia, Steven F. Bucky, and Sandra Wilder-Padilla. "The Interpersonal and Emotional Consequences of Being an Adult Child of an Alcoholic." *International Journal of the Addictions* 21(1986): 213-31.

Reports a study comparing adult children of alcoholics with adults raised in nonalcoholic homes on their perceptions of family history and problems, past and present drug and alcohol use, communication with significant others, physical and sexual abuse, and interpersonal differences experienced as adults. ACOAs reported more childhood family disruption, including physical and sexual abuse, than the comparison group and more emotional and psychological problems as adults. They also became alcoholic or married alcoholics more frequently than the children of the nonalcoholic group. References.

180.   Brisbane, Frances L. "The Family Hero in Black Alcoholism Families." *Journal of Alcohol and Drug Education* 34(Spring 1989): 29-37.

Describes findings from case studies of twenty Black adult female children of alcoholics. Data showed that the role of family hero in Black families was most likely to be held by the oldest or only Black female. The significance of race, culture, and gender in these findings is discussed along with the implications for treatment of these ACOAs. References.

181.   Claydon, Peter. "Self-Reported Alcohol, Drug, and Eating-Disorder Problems Among Male and Female Collegiate Children of Alcoholics." *Journal of American College Health* 36(1987): 111-16.

Reports findings of a study of incoming college freshmen to measure the proportion who were children of alcoholics. Determination was based on the use of self-reports and the Children of Alcoholics Screening Test. Information about the subjects' own drinking behaviors and problems with alcohol, drugs, or eating disorders was also solicited. Results showed that COAs were more likely to report substance abuse problems of their own. The author suggests the need for longitudinal research to identify those factors most closely associated with high risk for substance abuse and to improve diagnosis and intervention. References.

182.   Cutter, Constance G., and Henry S.G. Cutter. "Experience and Change in Al-Anon Family Groups: Adult children of Alcoholics." *Journal of Studies on Alcohol* 48(1987): 29-32.

Examines how adult children of alcoholics discuss their family experiences in an Al-Anon group and describes their perceptions of change in themselves, their personal problems, relationships, spiritual factors, childhood experiences, and the Al-Anon program. The study was based on observations of twelve consecutive sessions of an open Al-Anon adult children's group. Members reported positive changes in self and improvement in personal problems (20%) but few improvements in relationships with alcoholics. Socialization was suggested as a significant factor in members' improvement, whereas the concept of spirituality was difficult for many members to grasp (although seen as the most important component by a few). References.

183. Glenn, Susan W., and Oscar A. Parsons. "Alcohol Abuse and Familial Alcoholism: Psychosocial Correlates in Men and Women." *Journal of Studies on Alcohol* 50(1989): 116-27.

Discusses results of a study to identify psychosocial variables that may distinguish adult children of alcoholics from children of nonalcoholics and alcoholics from nonalcoholic controls. The study also examined whether differences in these groups are influenced by gender. The results indicated that alcohol abuse and family history of alcoholism are separate, distinct factors having additive but not interactional effects. No significant gender differences were found, which suggests that prior research on male alcoholics should be applicable to females as well. References.

184. Harford, Thomas C., Mary R. Haack, and Danielle L. Spiegler. "Epidemiologic Bulletin No. 18: Positive Family History for Alcoholism." *Alcohol Health and Research World* 12(1987/88): 138-43.

Uses data from a 1979 national drinking practices survey to examine the relationship between positive family history for alcoholism and the prevalence of alcohol consumption, alcohol-related problems, and alcohol dependence. Comparison of three groups--family history positive with alcoholic parents, family history positive with no alcoholic parents, and family history negative--found no significant differences in alcohol consumption. However, there was a greater level of alcohol-related problems and dependence among the family history positive groups as compared to the family history negative groups. Findings also showed that maternal alcoholism was clearly related to greater alcohol consumption and problems among adult offspring. References.

185.     Hesselbrock, Victor M., James O'Brien, Marlynn Weinstein, and Nancy Carter-Menendez. "Reasons for Drinking and Alcohol Use in Young Adults at High Risk and at Low Risk for Alcoholism." *British Journal of Addiction* 82(1987): 1335-39.

Examines relationship of attitudes toward use of alcohol and alcohol consumption among young adult children of alcoholics and children of nonalcoholic parents. No significant differences were found between the two groups on reasons for drinking or for limiting consumption. The family experience of ACOAs, suprisingly, did not appear to affect their attitudes toward alcohol use. References.

186.     Keltner, Norman L., Curtis W. McIntyre, and Ronald Gee. "Birth Order Effects in Second-Generation Alcoholics." *Journal of Studies on Alcohol* 47(1986): 495-97.

Analyzes findings of a study on relationship of birth order to development and severity of psychopathology among adult children of alcoholics. Subjects were inpatients in an alcoholism treatment program and all came from families of three children. Data was collected using the Minnesota Multiphasic Personality Inventory and the Shipley-Hartford Intelligence Scale, and results confirmed that middle- and last-born children were more likely to exhibit psychopathology than first-borns. Possible factors related to these differences are briefly discussed. References.

187.     Lincoln, Rosamund, and Elza Janze. "The Process of Recovery: Its Impact on Adult Children and

Grandchildren of Alcoholics." *Alcoholism Treatment Quarterly* 5, no. 1-2(1988): 249-59.

Measures the relationship between the degree of treatment and exposure to self-help groups and the codependency characteristics of adult children and grandchildren of alcoholics. Describes the development, testing, and use of a Co-Dependence Inventory (CCI) as a tool for measuring degrees of common codependence traits. References.

188. Parker, Douglas A., and Thomas C. Harford. "Alcohol-Related Problems of Children of Heavy-Drinking Parents." *Journal of Studies on Alcohol* 48(1987): 265-68.

Analyzes data from a 1978 household survey of employed adults in Detroit to determine relationship between heavy-drinking parents and dependent problem drinking in adult offspring. Adult children of heavy-drinking parents were found to have more problem drinking than those without heavy-drinking parents. Also adults in low status occupations had higher rates of problem drinking than those in higher status jobs. Results indicate that heavy-drinking parents and low status occupation put individuals at increased risk for alcohol problems. References.

189. Plescia-Pikus, Marlene, Emily Long-Suter, and John P. Wilson. "Achievement, Well-Being, Intelligence, and Stress Reaction in Adult Children of Alcoholics." *Psychological Reports* 62(1988): 603-9.

Examines achievement, well-being, intelligence, and stress reaction in a sample of adult children of alcoholics as compared to a control group of university students from nonalcoholic families. Adult COAs exhibited lower well-being and achievement over-all, but those with high well-being scored higher on achievement levels than controls or ACOAs with low well-being. Findings indicate that

fostering well-being within children may be the key for
helping them to cope successfully with an alcoholic family
system. References.

190.    Rearden, John J., and Becky S. Markwell. "Self-
        Concept and Drinking Problems of College Students
        Raised in Alcohol-Abused Homes." *Addictive
        Behaviors* 14(1989): 225-27.

        Surveys alcohol-related problems and self-concept of
college students using three instruments: the Michigan
Alcoholism Screening Test (MAST), the Children of
Alcoholics Screening Test (CAST), and the "personal self"
section of the Tennessee Self Concept Scale. Results
showed that 23% of students tested were children of
alcoholics, and the mean self-concept for these subjects
was lower than for the children of nonalcoholics. Although
31% of students demonstrated alcohol problems according to
their MAST scores, there was no significant correlation
between the MAST and CAST scores. Findings indicate that
college students would benefit from diagnostic programs as
well as short-term counseling to improve self-esteem and
increase awareness of the risks of heavy drinking.
References.

191.    Schuckit, Marc A., and Michael Irwin. "An Analysis
        of the Clinical Relevance of Type 1 and Type 2
        Alcoholics." *British Journal of Addiction* 84(1989):
        869-76.

        Examines the use of alcoholic subtypes in predicting
drinking patterns of adult male offspring. Subjects' fathers
were all diagnosed as primary alcoholics and were measured
on a subtype continuum to determine degree of type 2
alcoholism (characterized by earlier onset of alcohol
problems, history of violence with and without alcohol use,
and greater chance of involvement with other drugs).
Subjects themselves had not exhibited signs of alcohol
abuse or dependence prior to the study. Contrary to

expectations, subjects whose fathers scored higher on the type 2 continuum did not exhibit earlier onset of drinking or related problems. Authors discuss methodological problems inherent in this type of research as well as the possible influence of preexisting psychiatric disorder. References.

192.    Schuckit, Marc A., and Susan Sweeney. "Substance Use and Mental Health Problems Among Sons of Alcoholics and Controls." *Journal of Studies on Alcohol* 48(1987): 528-34.

Analyzes data from a survey of university male students and nonacademic staff aged 21-25 years to explore the relationship between substance use patterns and problems and family history of depression and substance abuse. Findings showed that only a small percentage of subjects met criteria for alcoholism or drug abuse. However, there was a significant increase in the number of minor alcohol and drug problems among men with family history of alcoholism in both first- and second-degree relatives as compared with subjects reporting no family alcoholism or alcoholism in first- or second-degree relatives only. There were no significant differences related to family history of psychiatric disorders. References.

193.    Webster, Daniel W., Ernest Harburg, Lillian Gleiberman, Anthony Schork, and Wayne DiFranceisco. "Familial Transmission of Alcohol Use: I. Parent and Adult Offspring Alcohol Use Over 17 Years--Tecumseh, Michigan." *Journal of Studies on Alcohol* 50(1989): 557-66.

Examines the relationship between parental drinking and the drinking patterns of adult offspring. Data on parents' drinking practices was gathered in 1960 as part of a longitudinal health study in Tecumseh, Michigan; their adult offspring were surveyed in 1977. Comparison of the self-reported drinking practices of the two groups showed a positive association between drinking level of parents and adult offspring. However, this association varied according to parental drinking level, sex of offspring, and sex of parent. The strongest correlation was found with abstaining parents, who tended to rear children that became abstainers or light drinkers. In addition, drinking patterns were compared to determine high-maximum (several drinks per occasion most of the time) or low-maximum (drinks consumed on a regular, spaced basis) drinking. Sons with fathers or two parents who exhibited high-maximum drinking were more likely to show the same drinking patterns. References.

194.    Williams, Karen F., and Steven B. Robbins. "New Study Casts Doubt on 'Roles' of Adult Children of Alcoholics." *Addiction Letter* 3(October 1987): 1-2.

        Describes findings of a study to test the notion that adult children of alcoholics engage in role behavior. A group of 120 ACOAs were identified using the Children of Alcoholics Screening Test, and these were compared to 120 non-ACOAs using self-report inventories. The results did not support the notion of a typology of ACOA roles and suggested that ACOAs may not differ significantly from non-ACOAs. Possible weaknesses in methodology of the study are identified, suggesting the need for further research in this area.

195.    Wilson, Sandra D. "Evangelical Christian Adult Children of Alcoholics: A Preliminary Study." *Journal of Psychology and Theology* 17(1989): 263-73.

        Compares personality characteristics and religious problems of evangelical Christian adult children of alcoholics with a control group of adult children of nonalcoholics from the same evangelical congregations. Three instruments were used to gather personal data and family history, to measure personality characteristics, and to determine parental alcoholism. ACOAs were found to be more depressed, distrusting, and self-blaming than the control group, and they also experienced more religious problems such as difficulty experiencing God's love and forgiveness. Results indicate that evangelical ACOAs demonstrate similar characteristics to ACOAs in the general population and that they are not protected from these problems by their religious practices. References.

196.     Workman-Daniels, Kathryn L., and Victor M. Hesselbrock. "Childhood Problem Behavior and Neuropsychological Functioning in Persons at Risk for Alcoholism." *Journal of Studies on Alcohol* 48(1987): 187-93.

Examines the relationship of childhood hyperkinetic and minimal brain dysfunction (Hk-MBD) to neuropsychological functioning in young adults at high risk for alcoholism. Nonalcoholic children of alcoholic parents were compared to nonalcoholic children of nonalcoholic parents and to a group of similar-aged alcoholic patients. The nonalcoholic ACOAs could not be distinguished from their nonalcoholic counterparts on the basis of cognitive abilities or frequency of childhood Hk-MBD symptoms. However, the alcoholic subjects did perform more poorly on certain verbal and performance measures and reported more childhood problem behavior symptoms. Findings did not suggest that certain cognitive deficits could distinguish persons with a positive family history for alcoholism, but poor neuropsychological functioning in adulthood did appear to be related to childhood Hk-MBD. References.

See also: 23, 30-31, 33, 114, 135, 197, 261, 276.

## 8. FAMILY ISSUES

### Books and Pamphlets

In this chapter the entries focus on describing how individuals' feelings and behaviors as adults may have been influenced by growing up in an alcoholic home. The materials cover such problems as low self-esteem, over-responsibility, inability to trust, fear of intimacy, poor parenting skills, and marital difficulties. Personal stories about childhood or adult experiences are included as well as materials focusing on codependency. Items dealing primarily with adults' recovery from parental alcoholism are found in chapter 10, **Adult Children: Recovery.**

197. Ackerman, Robert J. **Perfect Daughters: Adult Daughters of Alcoholics.** Deerfield Beach, FL: Health Communications, 1989. 197 pp.

Examines the effects on adult daughters of growing up with an alcoholic parent. Analyzes the responses from two surveys of women from alcoholic and nonalcoholic families to compare perceptions and problems related to family background. Explores problems of childhood development, including different effects associated with the sex of the alcoholic parent. Discusses current problems such as codependent behavior, parenting skills, and trouble with intimate relationships and offers suggestions to improve self-acceptance and self-esteem. Statistics from the

two research studies are presented in the appendix. Useful
for therapists as well as adult children. References.

198.    Ackerman, Robert J., ed. **Growing in the Shadow:**
        **Children of Alcoholics.** Deerfield Beach, FL: Health
        Communications, 1986. 234 pp.

Includes contributions from twenty-two authorities
on the needs and problems of children of alcoholics. Part
one of the text looks at how alcoholism affects the family
situation, including chapters on domestic violence and on
alcoholism in special minority families (Blacks, Hispanics,
and Native Americans). Part two examines the effects of
parental alcoholism on the development of young children,
while part three focuses on the problems experienced by
adolescent children from alcoholic homes. In part four the
special needs of adult children are discussed. Chapters
cover therapeutic issues and techniques as well as
professional issues engendered by ACOAs who enter the
alcoholism field. Written for counselors and ACOAs.
References.

199.    Anderson, Louie. **Dear Dad: Letters from an Adult**
        **Child.** New York: Viking Penguin, 1989. 209 pp.

Recounts the author's experiences growing up in a
family of eleven children with an alcoholic father. The
author, now a well-known comedian, uses a series of
letters written to his dead father to help him understand
his father's behavior and how it has affected his own life,
including his problem with overeating. Illustrations.

200.    Balis, Susan A. **Beyond the Illusion: Choices for**
        **Children of Alcoholics.** Deerfield Beach, FL: Health
        Communications, 1989. 205 pp.

Describes the negative psychological and emotional
effects of growing up in an alcoholic family in terms of
"illusions" that help children cope with an erratic,

dysfunctional family situation. Uses personal histories to elaborate on the variety of coping mechanisms, such as denial and rationalization, that contribute to the development of an illusion of normal family life. Explores how this illusion of strength and normalcy can disintegrate in adulthood, frequently leading to self-destructive behaviors and inability to cope with family situations. Discusses strategies for change, emphasizing the importance of both behavioral and personality change. Useful for adult children of alcoholics and therapists who work with this population. Bibliography.

201. Clarke, Jean I., and Connie Dawson. **Growing Up Again: Parenting Ourselves, Parenting Our Children.** Center City, MN: Hazelden, 1989. 183 pp.

Offers guidelines to help adults improve their parenting skills and avoid unhealthy behaviors that their own parents may have used. Includes a number of examples of alcohol or drug abuse in family situations. Explains the importance of structure as well as flexibility in parenting and emphasizes the need for unconditional love (nurturing) between parents and children and between adults themselves. Discusses the problems of denial that keep parents stuck in family problems and suggests ways of replacing denial with positive messages and behaviors. Also identifies seven developmental stages from birth to independent adulthood and describes helpful parent behaviors and activities that can contribute to personal and family growth. Especially helpful for family therapists or for adult children of alcoholics who need to develop their own self-esteem and to learn about positive parenting. Appendixes contain activities to coordinate with the text. References, bibliography, index.

202. Dean, Amy E. **What Is Normal? Family Relationships.** Center City, MN: Hazelden, 1988. 31 pp.

Identifies six areas of family interactions and illustrates how these differ between healthy and unhealthy families. Defines unhealthy families as those in which there is alcoholism, drug addiction, mental illness, physical or sexual abuse, or some other compulsive behavior or disruption that results in a non-nurturing environment. Discusses how such an environment may continue to affect children into their adult lives and offers practical suggestions to help adult children develop a strong sense of self and improve communication with family members.

203.    Deutsch, Charles. **For the One in Eight** Americans **Who Is the Child of an Alcoholic.** New York: Children of Alcoholics Foundation, 1986. 5 pp.

Written to help adult children of alcoholics understand the psychological and emotional effects that often result from growing up in an alcoholic home. Describes some behavior patterns commonly found among ACOAs, including difficulties in intimate relationships, overresponsibility, depression, and alcoholism. Uses several brief case histories to illustrate such problems and suggests resources to deal with them. Bibliography.

204.    Friel, John, and Linda Friel. **Adult Children: The Secrets of Dysfunctional Families.** Deerfield Beach, FL: Health Communications, 1988. 198 pp.

Examines the problems commonly suffered by adults who grew up in families where there was chemical dependence, workaholism, physical or sexual abuse, or other dysfunctional situations. Describes the physical and emotional symptoms and consequences with case examples to illustrate. Uses family systems theory to explain the dynamics of dysfunctional family behaviors and concludes with a brief section that outlines a general recovery program based on a twelve-step approach. Written for adult children. References.

205.   LeBoutillier, Megan. **Little Miss Perfect.** Denver:
MAC Publishing, 1987. 140 pp.

Uses the author's personal experiences to illustrate
the development of emotional and behavioral problems in
adult children of alcoholics. Focuses on the problem of
intimacy, which is often hindered in ACOAs by the fear of
vulnerability and the urge to assume the primary
responsibility for any relationship. Defines "Little Miss
Perfect" as the ACOA's need to be in control while
suppressing feelings of guilt and anxiety. Suggests steps for
building intimacy skills and identifies roadblocks that may
inhibit ACOAs from reaching the desired goal of
experiencing spontaneity and creative potential. Concludes
with suggested exercises for recovery such as journal-
keeping, meditation, daily affirmations, and creative
visualization. Bibliography includes books on ACOAs as well
as general self-help and wellness.

206.   Lee, John. **The Flying Boy: Healing the Wounded
Man.** Deerfield Beach, FL: Health Communications,
1987. 111 pp.

Explores special problems that may be experienced
by males who grew up with alcoholic fathers. Discusses
how men may reject the masculinity exemplified by
alcoholic fathers, resulting in a fear of commitment and
intimacy as well as a lack of male friendships. The author
uses his own personal experiences to illustrate the need for
understanding the past and grieving the loss of normal
childhood and family life. Written for male ACOAs and for
women who love them.

207.   Mastrich, Jim, with Bill Birnes. **The ACOA's Guide
to Raising Healthy Children: A Parenting Handbook
for Adult Children of Alcoholics.** New York: Collier
Books, 1988. 271 pp.

Offers practical suggestions to guide adult children
of alcoholics in raising healthy, well-adjusted children of

their own. The authors discuss the parenting problems that ACOAs frequently encounter as a result of their own dysfunctional childhoods and lack of understanding of normal family relationships. The text is written in chronological format to follow the developmental stages of childhood from birth to adulthood. For each stage parents are advised on the types of behaviors, activities, and relationships to encourage in their children. Suggestions for dealing with inappropriate behaviors (by parent or child) are also provided. In addition, there are guidelines for discussing alcohol and drug use with children and for preventing substance abuse problems. The final chapters cover special issues such as coping with change (through death or divorce) in the family, dealing with recovering or active alcoholic parents, and intervening as a grandparent in youthful alcohol or drug abuse. This book is a well-written, useful tool for ACOAs who are considering parenting or who have already started families. The appendix lists resource organizations, hotlines, and books on alcoholism and addiction, ACOAs, parenting, personal growth, relationships, and dealing with older parents. Bibliography, index.

208.    Middelton-Moz, Jane. **Children of Trauma: Rediscovering Your Discarded Self.** Deerfield Beach, FL: Health Communications, 1989. 185 pp.

Uses case histories to illustrate some of the emotional, behavioral, and physical problems that may be experienced by persons who suffered childhood trauma such as parental alcoholism, sexual abuse, verbal abuse, or neglect. Focuses on the importance of the developmental stages of childhood and demonstrates the negative effects that trauma has on emotional development, self-image, and ability to sustain healthy relationships. Useful for ACOAs and therapists. Bibliography.

209.  Reddy, Betty. **Alcoholism: A Family Illness.** Park
      Ridge, IL: Parkside Medical Services Corp., 1987.
      12 pp.

      Describes alcoholism as a family illness that affects
the feelings and behaviors of each family member in
addition to the alcoholic. Includes a section on children of
alcoholics and adult children, focusing on defense
mechanisms and coping patterns they develop to deal with
parental alcoholism. Concludes with a twenty-question
self-test to determine the existence of alcoholism within a
family and the extent of negative effects on an individual.
Recommends a self-help program such as Al-Anon to aid in
recovery of family members from the trauma of alcoholism.
Good introductory material for adult family members.

210.  Rolfe, Randy C. **Adult Children Raising Children:
      Sparing Your Child from Co-Dependency Without
      Being Perfect Yourself.** Deerfield Beach, FL: Health
      Communications, 1989. 196 pp.

      Identifies many of the problems that adult children
of alcoholics may encounter in raising their own children.
Describes some of the roles and behaviors ACOAs may have
learned as children and discusses how these may influence
their parenting skills and relationships with their children.
Offers detailed suggestions for improving communication,
trust, and understanding between parent and child.
Glossary, bibliography.

211.  Smith, Ann W. **Grandchildren of Alcoholics: Another
      Generation of Co-Dependency.** Deerfield Beach, FL:
      Health Communications, 1988. 168 pp.

      Discusses the psychological and emotional problems
that may be suffered by individuals who were raised by
parents that were children of alcoholics. Explains how the
dynamics of the dysfunctional family may be passed on by
adult children of alcoholics to their children, who are
often unaware of the alcoholism in the family. Identifies

family patterns and characteristics common to grandchildren of alcoholics and describes treatment options and self-help available for this population. Concludes with chapters outlining the stages of recovery and guidelines to change family patterns for a healthier lifestyle. References.

212.    Somers, Suzanne. **Keeping Secrets.** New York: Warner Books, 1988. 297 pp.

Tells the true story of the traumatic life of actress Suzanne Somers, who grew up with an alcoholic father. Depicts the erratic behavior and frequent episodes of violence exhibited by her father and shows the negative effects (including bed wetting, poor concentration, and further violence) on the author and her siblings as children. Describes the author's problems in adult life with self-esteem, intimate relationships, and finances, and relates these--as well as the alcohol and drug problems of her brothers and sister--to the inability to understand the disease of alcoholism and its effects on the family. The book concludes with a real-life happy ending that offers inspiration for all families. Suitable for adult family members or mature teens.

213.    Stuart, Mary S. **In Sickness and in Health: The Co-Dependent Marriage.** Deerfield Beach, FL: Health Communications, 1989. 114 pp.

Describes the characteristics of a healthy marriage and shows how these may be adversely affected by the codependency of one or both partners. Defines codependency as a reaction to growing up in a family in which there was alcoholism or other dysfunction. Identifies the major character traits and behavior patterns of codependents and provides examples of these patterns in codependent marital relationships. Concludes with a brief chapter of advice to help improve relationships through an emphasis on self-esteem and personal growth. The appendix contains a list of organizations for further help. Bibliography.

214. Subby, Robert. **Lost in the Shuffle: The Co-Dependent Reality.** Deerfield Beach, FL: Health Communications, 1987. 142 pp.

Provides insight to the feelings and problems of being a recovering alcoholic as well as an adult child from an alcoholic family. The author uses personal experiences to help illustrate the development and consequences of codependency--the denial of an individual's true feelings and reality in order to cope with family dysfunction. Discusses codependency in terms of a disease with stages progressing from compulsive behavior patterns through severe mental or emotional disturbance. Concludes with a short section on recovery issues with some suggested exercises such as "journalizing" feelings and experiences.

215. V., Rachel. **Family Secrets: Life Stories of Adult Children of Alcoholics.** San Francisco: Harper and Row, 1987. 260 pp.

Tells the personal stories of fifteen adults who grew up with alcoholic parents. The stories recount the painful experiences and the family roles played by the subjects and demonstrate how these factors affected adult feelings and behaviors. Each of the stories also describes how the subject entered recovery for the effects of family alcoholism or for his or her own substance abuse. In addition, there are discussions with poet Robert Bly and analyst Marion Woodman on letting go of past experiences and on the nature of addiction and spirituality, as well as brief remembrances of Lois W. and Bob S., Jr., on the early days of Alcoholics Anonymous and Al-Anon. Appendixes include an annotated list of resource organizations, the Twelve Steps and Twelve Traditions of Alcoholics Anonymous and Al-Anon, and Twelve Steps of Recovery for ACOA groups. Bibliography.

216.   Wegscheider-Cruse, Sharon. Co-Dependency: An
       **Illness, Describable and Treatable.** Rapid City, SD:
       Nurturing Networks, 1984. 36 pp.

       Defines codependency in terms of a preoccupation
with, and extreme dependence on, another person
(emotionally or physically). Identifies those groups of
people most likely to suffer from codependency, particularly
spouses and children of alcoholics. Describes the symptoms
of codependency--denial, compulsive behavior, repression of
feelings--and discusses some of the possible complications,
including low self-worth and stress-related medical
problems. The last section of the text focuses on the
emotional problems of adult children of alcoholics and
offers practical suggestions to help ACOAs face their
problems and learn how to change their behaviors. There is
also a helpful section written for parents of ACOAs who
want to help their children recover from the effects of
growing up in an alcoholic home. Useful for ACOAs, other
family members, and therapists working with this
population.

217.   Woititz, Janet G. **Adult Children of Alcoholics.** rev.
       ed. Deerfield Beach, FL: Health Communications,
       1990. 135 pp.

       Identifies thirteen "generalizations" regarding the
emotional and psychological functioning of adults who grew
up in alcoholic homes. Covers such topics as difficulty with
intimate relationships, impulsive behavior, and constant
need for approval. Includes suggestions for dealing with
negative feelings and established behavior patterns. This
book would be useful for adult children and for counselors
dealing with this population.

218.   Woititz, Janet G. **Adult Children of Alcoholics:
       Common Characteristics.** Deerfield Beach, FL: Health
       Communications, 1983. 12 pp.

Briefly discusses some of the most common behaviors and characteristics of adult children of alcoholics. Emphasizes the role of childhood experience in an alcoholic home in contributing to negative behaviors and self-image in adulthood.

219.    Woititz, Janet G. **Struggle for Intimacy.** Deerfield Beach, FL: Health Communications, 1985. 101 pp.

Written to help adult children of alcoholics identify the fears that may be causing difficulty in intimate relationships. Examines some relationship issues shared by ACOAs, such as fear of loss of self, fear of abandonment, anger, guilt and shame, and unrealistic expectations. There is a chapter on sexual issues in homosexual and heterosexual relationships, including a section on problems stemming from incest in childhood. There is also a chapter directed at the partners of ACOAs that offers helpful suggestions in dealing with hidden fears that create obstacles in relationships. The book concludes with a description of some common characteristics of ACOAs. Bibliography.

220.    Wolter, Dwight L. **A Life Worth Waiting For!** Minneapolis: CompCare, 1989. 243 pp.

Uses poetry and short personal vignettes to describe the author's life with his alcoholic parents and his steps toward recovery. Includes incidents and impressions from childhood as well as examples of how adult behaviors and feelings have been influenced by an alcoholic family situation. Also explores parenting issues that the author has encountered with his own child. In the final part of the text, the author demonstrates how he has learned to deal with many of the above problems and has developed a new, healthier lifestyle based on understanding and self-forgiveness.

## Journal Articles

221.   Adams, Kenneth M. "Sexual Addiction and Covert Incest: Connecting the Family Roots of Alcoholism, Neglect and Abuse." *Focus on Chemically Dependent Families* 10(May-June 1987): 10-11, 46.

Describes covert incest in which sexual contact does not actually take place but the feelings and dynamics are present. Identifies this as a significant factor in the development of sexual addiction by many adult children of alcoholics.

222.   Baasel, Patricia. "Co-Dependent Parents: Passing Down the Heritage of Addictive Family Dynamics." *Focus on Family and Chemical Dependency* 9(Nov.- Dec. 1986): 24-25, 36, 39.

Identifies the ways in which codependent behavior may affect the parenting skills of adult children of alcoholics. Outlines a "codependent parenting cycle" that moves from overinvolvement and overcontrolling, through anger, withdrawal (from rebellious children), and guilt, and then back to renewed efforts of control. Identifies the advantages and limitations of support groups to deal with parenting issues.

223.   Bratton, Mary, and Chris Galvin. "Inside the House of Mirrors: Blurred Boundaries and Identity Confusion in the Alcoholic Family." *Focus on Chemically Dependent Families* 11(Aug.-Sept. 1988): 24-25.

Discusses the dual personalities and identity confusion that frequently characterize alcoholic families. Discusses how the behavior patterns of family members are based on reactions to the alcoholic and examines how these patterns can affect subsequent adult behaviors and feelings in children of alcoholics.

224.    Graham, Hugh D. "The Paradox of Eleanor
        Roosevelt: Alcoholism's Child." *Virginia Quarterly
        Review* 63(1987): 210-30.

Describes the turbulent, lonely childhood of Eleanor
Roosevelt and discusses how this influenced her personal
and public life as an adult. Examines the close
relationship between the shy Eleanor and her charming,
adoring father who died tragically of alcoholism when she
was a young girl. Describes the stern and unloving
atmosphere in which Eleanor was raised by her maternal
grandmother and suggests how this family background may
have affected her ability to trust and to find fulfillment in
her own marriage and children. Discusses the common
behavioral roles that adult children of alcoholics often
manifest and demonstrates how Eleanor's actions
encompassed the roles of both the lost child and the hero.
Attributes much of the energy and dedication that Eleanor
displayed in her public causes to her need to bolster her
self-esteem and establish her identify through the eyes of
others.

225.    Hunt, Stephen C., and Regina A. Delmastro. "The
        Body Cries: Medical Consequences of Growing Up in
        an Alcoholic Family." *Focus on Family and Chemical
        Dependency* 8(July-Aug. 1985): 24-25.

Identifies some of the physical problems that adult
children of alcoholics frequently display and describes how
such problems may be related to growing up in a
dysfunctional family. Discusses how the unresolved stress
of living in a family situation characterized by
inconsistency, fear, anger, and abuse can lead to serious
medical, emotional, and psychological consequences in
adulthood. Suggests counseling for family alcohol issues to
help alleviate some physical symptoms.

226.    Hunter, Mic, and Terry Kellogg. "Characteristics of
        ACoAs: Seeking a Sense of Balance on the

Continuum of Inconsistency." *Focus on Chemically
Dependent Families* 10(May-June 1987): 26-27, 35.

Argues that the characteristics of adult children of
alcoholics should be seen as a continuum reflecting many
opposite attitudes and behaviors. Using thirteen commonly
identified characteristics, the authors demonstrate how
ACOA behaviors may vacillate between opposite extremes,
and they discuss the importance of understanding this
continuum for ACOAs in recovery.

227.    Larsen, Earnie. "Race Against Yesterday: The Ups
        and Downs of Intimacy for ACOAs." *Focus on
        Family and Chemical Dependency* 8(July-Aug. 1985):
        10-11, 44.

Presents a case history of two adult children from
alcoholic families who have sought counseling to help their
relationship. Their difficulties include a sense of alienation,
shame and guilt, fear of abandonment, and feelings of
unworthiness. The counselor demonstrates briefly how these
problems may be related to patterns learned while growing
up in an alcoholic home.

228.    Neikirk, John O. "Workaholism: The Pain Others
        Applaud." *Focus on Chemically Dependent Families*
        11(Aug.-Sept. 1988): 18-19, 39-41, 46.

Describes some of the common manifestations of
workaholism (compulsive working) and discusses why adult
children of alcoholics are at high risk for this problem.
Relates many of the characteristics of ACOAs, such as low
self-worth and an overdeveloped sense of responsibility, to
the need to excel in the workplace and suggests that
support groups or individual therapy will be needed to
change these feelings and behavior patterns.

229.    O'Gorman, Patricia, and Philip Oliver-Diaz.
        "Parenting in the Dark: Special Conditions for

ACoAs." *Focus on Chemically Dependent Families*
10(May-June 1987): 14-15, 18-19, 32-34.

Discusses why many adult children from alcoholic
families have poor parenting skills. Identifies some common
problems--such as hypervigilance, anxiety, jealousy, and
control--that ACOAs may experience in dealing with their
children and offers some basic rules for making positive
changes.

230.  Serkin, Elizabeth. "Elderly Alcoholics and Their
      Adult Children: Stereotypes and Other Obstacles to
      Treatment." *Focus on Chemically Dependent Families*
      10 (Sept.-Oct. 1987): 12-13, 23-25, 39.

Explains why many elderly alcoholics go undiagnosed
by professionals and by their own adult children. Describes
the burden on many adult children of dealing with aging
parents and trying to identify the source of harmful
behaviors. Because many of these alcoholics developed their
problem late in life, their adult children are usually
unfamiliar with the symptoms and the effects on the family
members, and they generally do not show up in self-help
groups or therapists' offices.

231.  Subby, Robert. "Lost in the Shuffle: Family
      Foundations of Co-Dependent Reality." *Focus on
      Chemically Dependent Families* 10(Mar.-Apr. 1987):
      6-7, 36, 46.

Defines codependency in terms of behavior patterns
that an individual acquires to cope with a dysfunctional
family system. Identifies four types of troubled family
systems from which codependency is likely to evolve,
including chemically dependent families. Describes several
problems which are common to many codependents, such as
perfectionism, rigidity, difficulty with intimacy, and low
self-esteem, and demonstrates how these problems develop
over time and contribute to unhappiness in adulthood.

232.    "To Help Substance Abusers, We Must First Help
        Ourselves." *Educational Leadership* 45(March 1988):
        21-22, 24-26.

   Discusses the prevalence of adult children of
alcoholics in the educational profession. The author uses
his own life story to demonstrate how growing up in an
alcoholic family affected his personal and professional life
as a teacher, school counselor, and administrator. Describes
the denial and enabling that may be practiced by
educators, which inhibits their ability to identify and help
students from alcoholic homes. References, bibliography.

   See also: 10, 43-45, 48, 61-62, 64-66, 69, 71, 77, 83,
171, 180, 236, 240, 242, 244, 269, 277-78, 282, 292, 303-4,
308, 310-11, 316, 325, 330, 333, 339, 345, 347.

# 9. TREATMENT

## Books and Pamphlets

The literature in this chapter is intended primarily for trained professionals working with adult children of alcoholics. There are items describing therapeutic approaches toward a variety of problems suffered by adult children as well as materials designed for use by employee assistance personnel. Literature written for adult children, to help them deal with their personal problems, is found in chapter 10, **Adult Children: Recovery.**

233.  Brown, Stephanie. **Treating Adult Children of Alcoholics: A Developmental Perspective.** New York: John Wiley and Sons, 1988. 333 pp.

Presents an in-depth, complex exploration of the links between growing up with an alcoholic parent and subsequent disturbances in adult functioning. The text is divided into three parts that focus on the alcoholic family environment, the effects of parental alcoholism on individual development, and the process of recovery from childhood trauma and its effects (including alcohol or drug abuse) for adult children of alcoholics. The author advocates a recovery process that is developmental and integrates cognitive, behavioral, and dynamic interventions. Emphasis is on core issues such as attachment, identity formation, trust, and separation. The text is intended primarily for therapists dealing with ACOAs or for other professionals--physicians, educators, employers--who often are in contact with ACOAs but lack the skills to identify or to intervene with these clients. However, there are numerous clinical examples (personal stories) that may be of benefit to ACOAs themselves, particularly those who have some knowledge of family or systems theory. Includes a brief review of the research literature on children of alcoholics. References and index.

234.    Brown, Stephanie, Susan Beletsis, and Timmen Cermak. **Adult Children of Alcoholics in Treatment.** Deerfield Beach, FL: Health Communications, 1989. 72 pp.

Presents three papers (previously published as journal articles) on important aspects of the authors' work with adult children of alcoholics at the Stanford (California) Alcohol Clinic. The papers focus on clinical insights from interactional group therapy with ACOAs, the developmental experience of ACOAs and its treatment through the group process, and the role of family transference as a therapeutic tool in ACOA groups. References.

235.    Cermak, Timmen L. **Diagnosing and Treating Co-Dependence: A Guide for Professionals Who Work with Chemical Dependents, Their Spouses and Children.** Minneapolis: Johnson Institute Books, 1986. 112 pp.

Offers practical advice to professionals who work with chemically dependent families. Focuses on the needs and problems suffered by codependents, who are defined as family members suffering from personality dysfunction related to one member's alcohol or drug abuse. Presents a set of criteria for diagnosing codependent personality disorder and provides clinical examples to illustrate how these criteria may be recognized in clients. There is a brief section on special problems of children and adult children of alcoholics, including post-traumatic stress disorder, psychic numbing, hypervigilance, and survivor guilt. The book concludes with guidelines for treating co-dependence. The recovery process is divided into four stages, and the major goals for each stage are discussed. References, index.

236. **Co-Dependency.** Deerfield Beach, FL: Health Communications, 1988. 98 pp.

Presents contributions of twelve experts in treating families of alcoholics. All of the chapters focus on co-dependency as the illness that develops in families centered on one member's addiction or dysfunctional behavior. Examines roles played by family members as well as developmental issues related to children of alcoholics. Written for family therapists and others who work with spouses and adult children of alcoholics.

237. **Co-Dependency: Issues in Treatment and Recovery.** Binghamton, NY: Haworth Press, 1989. 167 pp.

Offers advice from clinicians on a variety of issues related to codependency. Covers definitions and assessment of codependence, system dynamics in alcoholic families, family roles, and treatment of codependence, as well as an article devoted specifically to the use of education, support, and psychotherapy in recovery for adult children of alcoholics (see item 275). Also published as *Alcoholism Treatment Quarterly* 6, no. 1(1989). References.

238. Curtin, Paul J. **Resistance and Recovery for Adult Children of Alcoholics.** Delaware Water Gap, PA: Quotidian, 1987. 87 pp.

Explores barriers to recovery of normal, healthy relationships for adult children of alcoholics. Identifies specific obstacles to recovery in marital and intimate relationships and also discusses problems of denial and other psychological or compulsive disorders. Intended for use in group therapy to encourage healthy interaction and breakdown of resistance to acceptance of past trauma and present consequences. Written as a follow-up to **Tumbleweeds** (item 239).

239.    Curtin, Paul J. **Tumbleweeds: A Therapist's Guide to Treatment of ACOAs.** Delaware Water Gap, PA: Quotidian, 1985. 87 pp.

Focuses on group therapy as a means of helping adult children of alcoholics develop healthy, intimate relationships. Describes how to use the group setting as a tool to help ACOAs learn to accept and express their emotions. Also examines problems of control issues and coping with separation. Written as a manual for counselors. References.

240.    Gorski, Terence T. **Do Family of Origin Problems Cause Chemical Addiction? Exploring the Relationship Between Chemical Dependence and Codependence.** Independence, MO: Herald House/Independence Press, 1989. 53 pp.

Offers discrete definitions for chemical dependency and codependency and discusses their relationship. Cites the work of several well-known researchers in the chemical dependency field to argue that codependence does not cause alcoholism but does interfere with recovery. Stresses that successful recovery from alcoholism requires a primary focus on the disease itself and presents practical guidelines for therapists who treat chemically dependent adult children of alcoholics. Bibliography.

241.    Harding, Frances M., and Leslie S. Connor. **Alcohol Problems Prevention/Intervention Programs: Guidelines for College Campuses.** rev. ed. Albany: New York State Division of Alcoholism and Alcohol Abuse, 1988. 114 pp.

Presents recommendations for developing college alcohol prevention programs. Provides background material on alcohol-related problems in general and the special needs of certain at-risk groups--children of alcoholics, women, and minority students. The chapter on COAs discusses the types of problem behaviors they may exhibit as well as their likelihood of developing alcoholism. The bulk of the text focuses on the steps needed to develop and implement an alcohol program. Chapters cover needs assessment, defining goals and objectives, establishing an alcohol policy, publicizing a campus prevention program, intervening with and referring troubled students, and program evaluation. The appendices include a sample needs assessment survey, an alcohol knowledge test, and sample guidelines and materials from the University of Maryland's Alcohol Education Program. Although this manual was designed by the state of New York for its college system, most statistics are national, and the guidelines could be easily adapted to other regions. References.

242.  McFarland, Barbara, and Tyeis Baker-Baumann. **Feeding the Empty Heart: Adult Children and Compulsive Eating.** San Francisco: Harper and Row, 1988. 106 pp.

Explores the relationship between compulsive eating (overeating and bulimia) and growing up in an alcoholic home. Identifies personality characteristics and family roles commonly adopted by children of alcoholics and relates these to the development of eating disorders in adolescence and adulthood. Offers guidelines for therapists treating ACOAs for compulsive eating and includes several case histories to illustrate developmental and treatment issues. There is also a brief list of organizations for further help. Tables, bibliography, index.

243.  Mansmann, Patricia A., and Patricia A. Neuhausel. **Life After Survival: A Therapeutic Approach for**

**Children of Alcoholics.** Malvern, PA: Genesis Publishing Co., 1986. 44 pp.

Designed for use as a therapeutic tool with adult children of alcoholics. Focuses on the stages of recovery as described by Gravitz and Bowden (item 308): survival, awareness, core issues, transformations, integration, and genesis (spiritual awakening). The text is based on an understanding of the ACOA syndrome and related issues, and it includes a list of suggested books, articles, tapes, and lectures that can provide the necessary background knowledge. Includes several screening instruments that can be used to assess personal and family alcohol problems. Bibliography.

244.    Perez, Joseph F. **Relationships: Adult** Children of **Alcoholics.** New York: Gardner Press, 1989. 159 pp.

Uses five case histories to illustrate how adults who grew up in alcoholic families often have difficulties in their personal relationships. Each case includes a description of the adult's presenting problem (alcoholism, marital problems, overeating, physical or sexual abuse) as told to the author, a practicing psychologist. In addition, the author explores the clients' family background, relating childhood experiences and development to current problems, and describes his own therapeutic advice and prognosis. He concludes with a brief chapter of "do's and dont's" to help ACOAs and their partners develop healthy interpersonal relationships.

245.    Richards, Tarpley, Martha Tuohey, and Patricia Petrash. **Children of Alcoholics: A Guide for Professionals.** South Laguna, CA: National Association for Children of Alcoholics, 1987. 35 pp.

Defines three types of groups--educational, support, and psychotherapeutic--that are used in the treatment of problems suffered by adult children of alcoholics. Describes the goals of these groups and compares them in terms of process, content, boundaries, and roles of leader and participant. Offers suggestions to help therapists evaluate clients for psychotherapeutic groups and uses case examples to illustrate the dynamics of group interaction. Includes a short list of resources for information about alcoholism and the family. References.

246.    Russell, Laura. **Child Abuse and Alcoholism: A Suggested Model for Future Research and Treatment.** Rutherford, NJ: Thomas W. Perrin, 1984. 20 pp.

Discusses the correlation between parental alcoholism and child abuse--both physical and sexual. Argues for a diagnosis of child abuse as post traumatic stress disorder, which must be treated in addition to other negative consequences of growing up in an alcoholic home. Offers suggestions to help abused children release their pain as adults and learn to construct healthy relationships with their own children. Written primarily for ACOAs and therapists.

247.    Tessmer, Kathryn. **Breaking the Silence: A Workbook for Adult Children of Alcoholics.** Santa Rosa, CA: A.C.A.T. Press, 1986. 134 pp.

Designed to help adult children of alcoholics through the first stage of recovery from the childhood trauma of family alcoholism. Intended for use primarily in ACOA therapy groups to help participants "break the silence" of denial by acknowledging and accepting repressed feelings such as anger, fear, guilt, and grief. Uses writing exercises about a fictional cat family to help group members express feelings and explore past family relationships and behaviors. Also includes a short chapter for group leaders that describes the goals of the workbook exercises. Group leaders should have previous training or experience with family alcohol problems. Bibliography, illustrations.

248.    Vannicelli, Marsha. **Group Psychotherapy with Adult Children of Alcoholics: Treatment Techniques and Countertransference Considerations.** New York: Guilford Press, 1989. 222 pp.

Advocates the use of interactional group therapy (as developed by I.D. Yalom, 1975) with adult children of alcoholics. Reviews the research and popular literature on adult children and describes how and why group therapy can be an effective tool with this population. Offers detailed guidelines for establishing and maintaining an ACOA group and explores some "leader issues" such as countertransference (a therapist's emotional reaction to a client) that can affect group and individual progress. This book is an excellent manual for therapists who have experience with ACOAs and/or group therapy. It provides the basic information needed to apply the interactional group approach to this specific client population. The appendixes include an alcohol and drug history questionnaire, the Michigan Alcoholism Screening Test, a list of group ground rules, and a clinical data sheet. References, bibliography, index.

249.    Wegscheider-Cruse, Sharon. **Another Chance: Hope and Health for the Alcoholic Family.** 2d ed. Palo Alto, CA: Science and Behavior Books, 1989. 324 pp.

Examines the changes that occur in a family when a member becomes alcoholic. Defines the roles taken on by individual family members in response to the needs and actions of the alcoholic and contrasts the functioning of an alcoholic family system to that of a healthy family. Presents guidelines to help counselors intervene to restore the alcoholic family to health and describes the process of family reconstruction (adopted from the work of Virginia Satir) as a valuable tool in the recovery of family members. Includes a chapter on the special problems of adult children of alcoholics, focusing on the symptoms and emotional consequences of codependency. Also discusses the problems of denial and codependency that may be found in helping professionals. Written for family therapists but may also be helpful for adult family members. Appendixes include suggested exercises to use in family or group therapy sessions and a checklist to help professionals evaluate their personal attitudes and professional effectiveness. Bibliography, index.

250. Wegscheider-Cruse, Sharon. **Choice-Making for Co-Dependents, Adult Children and Spirituality Seekers.** Deerfield Beach, FL: Health Communications, 1985. 206 pp.

Defines the illness of codependency as an extreme dependency on another person or object and discusses why this phenomenon is frequently exhibited by family members of an addicted person. Describes the most common behavioral and emotional signs of codependency, including low self-esteem, rigidity, extreme need for approval, and difficulty expressing feelings. Focuses on several groups that have a high incidence of codependency: young children of alcoholics, adult children of alcoholics, and helping professionals (doctors, counselors, community workers, etc.). The goals and benefits of family therapy dealing with addiction and codependency are discussed along with pitfalls to avoid during the early stages of recovery. Useful for counselors, health professionals, or social service workers as well as for families of alcoholics. References.

251. Weiss, Laurie, and Jonathan B. Weiss. **Recovery from Co-Dependency: It's Never Too Late to Reclaim Your Childhood.** Deerfield Beach, FL: Health Communications, 1989. 221 pp.

Uses the concepts of transactional analysis (TA) to identify and treat codependency problems among adult children of alcoholics or other dysfunctional families. Focuses on the unmet needs of the inner child as the roots of codependent behavior and offers a treatment model based on identifying and working through repressed feelings from various stages of childhood. Appropriate for therapists and clients involved in TA groups. Bibliography.

252.    Woititz, Janet G. **The Self-Sabotage Syndrome: Adult Children in the Workplace.** Deerfield Beach, FL: Health Communications, 1989. 126 pp.

Discusses problems frequently experienced by adult children of alcoholics in the workplace and offers suggestions to help counselors in employee assistance programs recognize and deal with these issues. Part one describes common characteristics and behaviors of ACOAs on the job, including workaholism and burnout. There are brief case histories of ACOAs in a variety of occupations with positions at different levels. In part two guidelines are presented to help counselors, as well as ACOAs themselves, counteract these negative behaviors by developing healthy workplace patterns and relationships. There is also a chapter that focuses on the obstacles often encountered by ACOAs who become professional counselors themselves. Formerly titled **Home Away From Home.** Bibliography.

253.    Woodside, Migs. **Children of Alcoholics on the Job: Report for Health Care and Human Resource Professionals in Corporations and Employee Assistance Programs.** New York: Children of Alcoholics Foundation, 1986. 10 pp.

Identifies some of the problems that may be experienced by adult children of alcoholics and illustrates how these can affect performance in the workplace. Presents the results of a survey of corporate medical directors and employee assistance personnel to determine awareness of the problems and needs of ACOAs. Offers several specific recommendations for meeting the needs of ACOAs in the workplace, such as additional training for employee assistance staff and providing COA literature to employees. Concise and well-written overview intended for employee assistance or related personnel. Bibliography.

## Journal Articles

254. Balis, Susan A. "Illusion and Reality: Issues in the Treatment of Adult Children of Alcoholics." *Alcoholism Treatment Quarterly* 3(Winter 1986): 67-91.

Uses case histories to demonstrate the misleading images that adult children of alcoholics often present in treatment. Discusses the need for therapists to understand and break through such illusions in order for treatment to be effective.

255. Bratton, Mary. "Family Intervention: Tools for Getting Adult Children of Alcoholics to Treatment." *Focus on Chemically Dependent Families* 10(Jan.-Feb. 1987): 10-11.

Identifies some reasons why adult children of alcoholics may not seek treatment for themselves and suggests that they can receive help through a family intervention. Demonstrates how the information received by ACOAs during the training for an intervention can bring awareness of the negative effects family alcoholism has caused in their lives. Recommends that therapists be alert to the possible treatment needs of ACOAs who request help for a family member.

256. Brown, Stephanie, and Susan Beletsis. "Family Transference Development in Adult Children's Group Therapy: Re-Enactment of the Original Family Drama." *Focus on Chemically Dependent Families* 12(Aug.-Sept. 1989): 18-19, 38-43.

Discusses the dynamics of family transference in group therapy for adult children of alcoholics. Defines family transference as the "tendency to view the group as the family of origin and to behave in the group as one once did in that first family." Provides examples of individual behaviors within the group and discusses how these have led to group support and to the goal of detachment and separation from the group and the family of origin.

257.    Cameron-Bandler, Leslie. "Influencing Behavior in the Alcoholic Family: Strategies for Creating a Compelling Future." *Focus on Family and Chemical Dependency* 9(July-Aug. 1986): 6-7, 37, 44.

Describes a technique that can be used to enhance therapy for alcoholics and family members. This process, called "generating a compelling future," is discussed as one possible way to help adult children of alcoholics avoid developing alcoholism or similar problems. The objective of this process is to help the client imagine a positive future for him/herself and to identify and strengthen those behaviors and characteristics needed to attain that future.

258.    Chandler, Carole J. "ACAs: The Paradox and the Dilemma." *EAP Digest* 8(Nov.-Dec. 1987): 46-50, 86.

Identifies some of the positive and negative characteristics that adult children of alcoholics may exhibit in the workplace. Emphasizes the need to include services or referral for ACOAs in employee assistance programs and suggests ways of educating EAP personnel to recognize and deal more effectively with ACOA issues.

259.    Coyle, Patricia. "Vulnerability and Power in Group Therapy for ACOAs." *Focus on Family and Chemical Dependency* 8(July-Aug. 1985): 21, 27, 35.

Describes the paradoxical feelings of vulnerability and power that may characterize adult children of alcoholics and demonstrates how these feelings may be acted out in group therapy. Uses a case history to illustrate the importance of feedback and behavioral reactions of group members in helping ACOAs to understand their own behavior and its results more clearly. Identifies the goal of group therapy as helping ACOAs develop confidence and skills to effect positive changes in their behaviors and relationships.

260. Crandell, John S. "Brief Treatment for Adult Children of Alcoholics: Accessing Resources for Self-Care." *Psychotherapy* 26(1989): 510-12.

Suggests that not all adult children of alcoholics may need prolonged therapy in order to deal with problems stemming from family alcoholism. Argues that many ACOAs have the necessary strengths and character traits to help them function successfully but may need help in order to use these traits in their own behalf. Offers a case history to demonstrate how an ACOA was helped to use her skills in caring for others to develop a self-caring attitude. References.

261. Crawford, Robert L., and Ann Q. Phyfer. "Adult Children of Alcoholics: A Counseling Model." *Journal of College Student Development* 29(1988): 105-11.

Provides a framework for offering counseling services to adult children of alcoholics on the college campus. Describes the survival roles frequently adopted by COAs and discusses the various counseling roles that service providers may play in helping students through the progressive stages of recovery from the effects of parental alcoholism. Includes a review of current theory and literature on ACOAs and suggests areas of research needs. References.

262. Dean, Patricia R., and Tonya A. Edwards. "Adult Children of Alcoholics in Nursing." *EAP Digest* 9(Jan.-Feb. 1989): 41-44.

Discusses the prevalence of adult children of alcoholics among nurses and describes the impact on service delivery and the profession at large. Identifies common characteristics and behaviors of ACOA nurses and offers suggestions for preventing problems such as substance abuse among this population. Encourages the establishment of an employee assistance or peer assistance program to identify and help with problems at an early stage. References.

263.    Dean, R. Kent. "Post-Traumatic Stress Disorder in Adult Children of Alcoholics." *The Counselor* 6(July-Aug. 1988): 11-13.

Describes post-traumatic stress disorder as it may apply to the behavior of some adult children of alcoholics. Defines this phenomenon as an anxiety disorder that can develop as a result of the failure of coping strategies for dealing with parental alcoholism and other abuse (verbal, physical, sexual). Identifies some of the possible symptoms of this disorder in adults--including flashbacks, suicide attempts, and substance abuse--and offers suggestions for providing therapeutic support to help ACOAs work through the trauma.

264.    Fischer, Bruce. "The Process of Healing Shame." *Alcoholism Treatment Quarterly* 4(Summer 1987): 25-38.

Provides guidelines to help therapists deal with shame in adult children of alcoholics. Outlines nine stages of a healing process for internalized shame, which range from building a trusting relationship with the client to helping the client form a new identity based on feelings of self-esteem, self-worth, and capability. The process described may be used in individual, group, or family therapy or support groups. References.

265.   Henman, James O. "Conscious Competence and Other
       Paradoxes for Adult Children." *Focus on Chemically
       Dependent Families* 10(July-Aug. 1987): 12-13, 16,
       22, 33.

       Describes   adult   children   of   alcoholics   as
characterized by paradox--displaying adult behaviors that
mask   the   inner   feelings   of   helplessness   learned   from
childhood.   Introduces   a   therapeutic   approach,   termed
"cognitive perceptual reconstruction," based on the goal of
helping   the   client   to   internalize   self-respect   and   to
recognize and parent the repressed inner child.

266.   Jacobson, Steven B. "The 12-Step Program and
       Group Therapy for Adult Children of Alcoholics."
       *Journal of Psychoactive Drugs* 19(1987): 253-5.

       Illustrates   the   dynamics   and   techniques   of
supervised group therapy and twelve-step support group
programs   and   discusses   their   complementary   role   in   the
recovery   process   for   adult   children   of   alcoholics.   The
author advocates support group programs as the best way
of providing a safe environment to initiate newcomers into
the recovery process. He defines the role of the therapist
as   one   of   assessment   and   motivation   into   treatment   and
serving as the leader of therapy groups designed to help
ACOAs uncover the past and learn to cope in the present.
References.

267.   Kellogg, Terry, and John Friel. "ACoAs Meet EAPs:
       The Missing Link in Corporate Wellness Programs."
       *Focus on Chemically Dependent Families* 10(May-
       June 1987): 22-23, 29, 35.

       Argues   that   employee   assistance   programs   and
corporate wellness programs often ignore (or are unaware
of) problems of adult children of alcoholics at the
workplace. Describes a program designed to bring these
issues to the attention of all participants--management and
employees--in a corporate program.

268.    Kincade, Joan P. "The Wall of Words: Discovering Feelings Through Play Therapy." *Focus on Chemically Dependent Families* 10(Nov.-Dec. 1987): 12-13, 27.

Discusses the role of play in group therapy for adult children of alcoholics. Describes several types of play--including puppets, collages, drawing, and storytelling--and demonstrates their usefulness in helping ACOAs accept and release the feelings of the past.

269.    Levin, Paula B. "From Mother to Daughter: The Emotional Inheritance. Boundary Confusion and Loss of Self in the Alcoholic Family." *Focus on Chemically Dependent Families* 12(Aug.-Sept. 1989): 22-23, 29-31.

Advises therapists working with adult children of alcoholics to focus on building a strong, trusting relationship with their clients in order to help them effect lasting behavioral change. Emphasizes the need to examine clients' past histories to determine at what stage childhood development was arrested and to help ACOAs complete their emotional and behavioral growth.

270.    Levy, Frederick A. "Addicted Adult Children in Treatment: What Do You Deal With First?" *Focus on Chemically Dependent Families* 11(Feb.-Mar. 1988): 27-28.

Addresses obstacles often encountered by therapists when treating adult children of alcoholics who are chemically dependent. The author advises examining the emotional needs of the adult child to allow the client to realize the existence and depth of needs and to deal with feelings of loss. Suggests the use of autobiography and genograms as tools for uncovering clients' needs and breaking down resistance to treatment for chemical dependency.

271. Ponchalek, Karl, and Nancy C. Reynolds. "Intervening with Collegiate COAs: Can We Afford Not To?" *Journal of American College Health* 37(1988): 140-41.

Suggests that colleges and universities are in an important and favorable position to offer treatment services to students from alcoholic families. Argues that college attendance represents for most students both physical and emotional separation from parents which may precipitate crisis and make it easier to discuss and deal with underlying problems. Briefly describes the COA group therapy program at Cornell University and discusses its success in recruiting and helping students.

272. Potter-Efron, Patricia S. "Creative Approaches to Shame and Guilt: Helping the Adult Child of an Alcoholic." *Alcoholism Treatment Quarterly* 4(Summer 1987): 39-56.

Discusses shame and guilt as feeling experiences that have a powerful impact on adult children of alcoholics. Suggests therapeutic strategies to help ACOAs deal more effectively with shame and guilt through self-acceptance and improvement of self-image. References.

273. Rekers, Gail A., and John Hipple. "Co-Dependency Without Alcoholism? Teetotalers and the Family Transmission of Addiction." *Focus on Family and Chemical Dependency* 9(July-Aug. 1986): 18-20, 29.

Examines some of the problems that adult children of teetotalers may experience with their families and demonstrates how these problems may be related to alcohol problems in the grandparents' generation. Discusses patterns of family interaction in alcoholic families and shows how these may be perpetuated in the families of teetotaling offspring. Offers suggestions to help counselors recognize alcoholic family patterns in nonalcoholic families and provide assistance with parenting skills as well as individual and group therapy.

274.    Riccelli, Carlene. "Adult Children of Alcoholics on Campus: Programming for a Population at Risk." *Journal of American College Health* 36(1987): 117-22.

Describes a workshop program offered to adult children of alcoholics on campus by the Alcohol Education Program at the University of Massachusetts. The initial program consisted of four single-session workshops for students to discuss their concerns about family or individual problems and to develop coping skills to deal with the family environment. The program was expanded into a multi-session group program to respond to students' needs for more in-depth discussion of problems, coping strategies, and self-awareness. Recommendations are provided for college personnel who might want to establish similar programs. References.

275.    Richards, Tarpley M. "Recovery for Adult Children of Alcoholics: Education, Support, Psychotherapy." *Alcoholism Treatment Quarterly* 6, no. 1 (1989): 87-110.

Outlines three general categories of help for adult children of alcoholics--education and information, peer support, and psychotherapy--and uses case histories to demonstrate how these approaches may work with different clients and problems. Identifies several characteristics of an alcoholic home and discusses how the degree to which these are present may influence children's emotional development and subsequently affect adult behavior. References.

276.    Roush, Kristin L., and Richard R. DeBlassie. "Structured Group Counseling for College Students

of Alcoholic Parents." *Journal of College Student Development* 30(1989): 276-77.

Reports the findings of a study on the effect of structured group counseling on collegiate children of alcoholic parents. The experimental structured groups provided information about alcoholism and its effects on the family as well as a forum for the expression of feelings and the exploration of positive coping skills. Control groups received educational lectures only. Using pre- and post-testing, both experimental and control groups showed a significant increase in knowledge related to family alcoholism. However, only the experimental groups demonstrated healthier coping attitudes, and there were no significant improvements for behavior in any groups. Although more research is needed, findings indicate that group counseling can be an effective technique with college COAs. References.

277.   St. Anne, Jan. "Codependence and the Reaction Syndrome." *EAP Digest* 9(July-Aug. 1989): 37-42.

Provides advice for employee assistance personnel in dealing with problems of codependence that may be exhibited by spouses or adult children of alcoholics. Defines codependence in terms of a "reaction syndrome"-- negative behavior patterns that have developed as a reaction to the dysfunctional family situation. Claims that such reactions involve the suppression of true feelings and suggests that EAP counselors focus on helping codependents recognize their reaction patterns and learn to accept and express their feelings.

278.   Shulman, Gerald. "Co-Dependency: An Endangered Concept: Creating Coherence from Chaos and Confusion." *Focus on Chemically Dependent Families* 11(Aug.-Sept. 1988): 22-23, 32-33.

Discusses the difficulties in defining and diagnosing codependence and points out the problems that clients may encounter in seeking treatment for this disorder. Differentiates between codependency and psychiatric disorder and suggests that codependency should not be viewed as a unidimensional disorder. Briefly describes a number of variables that may affect an adult child's response to a dysfunctional family environment and recommends treatment personnel develop a more cohesive definition of codependency that includes a range of subtypes and which might be acceptable as a legitimate disorder by the medical community.

279. Stevens, Sally, and Roger Young. "Co-Dependency and Compulsive-Addictive Behavior: Obstacles to Recovery for Adult Children." *Focus on Family and Chemical Dependency* 8(July-Aug. 1985): 18-19.

Suggests that compulsive-addictive behaviors, such as gambling, overeating, and workaholism, are frequently present but unidentified in adult children of alcoholics. Uses brief case histories to demonstrate how individuals who have been treated for alcoholism or other addiction may continue to suffer from compulsive behaviors that were never identified as primary problems. Offers suggestions to therapists to help them recognize and understand the importance of dealing with such behaviors in ACOAs.

280. Sullivan-Chin, Margaret, and Jeffrey C. Chin. "Reaching Unseen Victims: Adult Children of Alcoholics." *EAP Digest* (May-June 1988): 51-52, 61-63, 88.

Presents general statistics and information for employee assistance personnel about children of alcoholics. Discusses family roles and how these may affect the work performance of adults who grew up with alcoholic parents. Offers some basic, practical suggestions to reach out to ACOAs on the job. References.

281.    Towns, Peyton. "Elephants in the Waiting Room: A Fable About Giving Up Our Blinders and Doing Therapy with Adult Children." *Focus on Chemically Dependent Families* 11(June-July 1988): 24-25, 41.

Discusses the differences in treatment approach among marriage and family therapists, sexual abuse therapists, and adult children (or codependency) therapists. Identifies the emphasis and limitations of each treatment approach as applied to therapy for adult children of alcoholics. Suggests that greater cooperation and education is needed for clinicians using these therapeutic approaches and offers guidelines to help ACOAs who are seeking a therapist.

282.    Weiss, Laurie, and Jonathan B. Weiss. "Retrieving the Lost Child Within: A Developmental Approach to Treatment for ACoAs." *Focus on Chemically Dependent Families* 10(Jan.-Feb. 1987): 14-15, 30-32, 36, 39.

Suggests that unmet needs in the developmental stages of children of alcoholic families are the foundation of many problems they experience in adulthood. Provides brief descriptions of these stages, showing the development that should occur and contrasting it with actual experience (or lack of experience) that may happen in alcoholic families. Outlines an intervention strategy for therapists based on a transactional analysis model of child development for identifying and fulfilling unmet needs.

283.    Wolkind, Beverly L. "A New Perspective on Adult Children of Alcoholics: Interview with Robert J. Ackerman, Ph.D." *EAP Digest* 7(Jan.-Feb. 1987): 25-29, 74.

Outlines some of the positive and negative behavior patterns that adult children of alcoholics frequently bring to the workplace and discusses why ACOAs may react differently to job stress. Recommends careful background screening by employee assistance professionals in order to determine those factors related to an ACOA's problems on the job and to help strengthen positive behavioral qualities that will contribute to job success. References.

See also: 8, 30, 79-80, 83, 97, 109, 114, 135, 151, 180, 187, 198, 225, 293, 300, 311, 317-18, 320, 337.

# 10. RECOVERY

## Books and Pamphlets

This chapter cites literature written for adult children themselves, to help them overcome problems in their adult lives that may have resulted from growing up with alcoholic parents. All of the entries provide some type of guidelines or techniques for dealing with adult problems such as difficulties with intimate relationships, workaholism, and codependency. Materials on self-help groups are included, but items dealing with other therapeutic approaches are found in chapter 9, **Adult Children: Treatment**. For further information on the effects of parental alcoholism on adult children, see chapter 8, **Adult Children: Family Issues**.

284. Ackerman, Robert J. **Let Go and Grow: Recovery for Adult Children.** Deerfield Beach, FL: Health Communications, 1987. 183 pp.

Identifies common personality characteristics shared by adult children and provides guidelines for recovery from the effects of growing up in an alcoholic home. Based on the study described in item 171 comparing perceptions and behaviors of ACOAs with adult children from nonalcoholic homes. Focuses on the adult child's personal assessment and understanding of family roles and other coping behaviors and offers insights for changing negative

149

behaviors into positive strengths. Useful for therapists as well as recovering ACOAs. Bibliography.

285. Al-Anon Family Groups. **Al-Anon Faces Alcoholism.** 2d ed. New York: Al-Anon Family Group Headquarters, 1985. 275 pp.

Discusses the Al-Anon program (for families of alcoholics) from three different perspectives. The first section contains articles from leading alcoholism treatment practitioners presenting their viewpoints on the value of Al-Anon and how they use it as a family recovery tool. The next section presents the stories of a variety of persons who were helped by the Al-Anon program. Several of these stories deal with persons who grew up in alcoholic homes, including stories by teenagers who have found help through Alateen groups. In the final section the Al-Anon program itself is described, including the Twelve Steps and Twelve Traditions. Index.

286. Al-Anon Family Groups. **Al-Anon Is for Adult Children of Alcoholics.** New York: Al-Anon Family Group Headquarters, 1983. 13 pp.

Briefly illustrates some of the most significant special problems experienced by adult children of alcoholics. Gives examples to show how each of the Twelve Steps in the Al-Anon program can be used to help these victims cope with their problems.

287. Al-Anon Family Groups. **Al-Anon Sharings** from **Adult Children.** New York: Al-Anon Family Group Headquarters, 1984. 17 pp.

Presents brief stories from fourteen adults with alcoholic parents. Describes how the Al-Anon program helped them deal with their parents' alcoholism and regain control over their own lives.

288. American College Health Association. **Adult Children of Alcohol Abusers.** Rockville, MD, 1988. 2 pp.

   Provides basic information and statistics on the feelings and problems experienced by college students who grew up with an alcoholic parent. Briefly outlines the different drinking patterns of social drinkers, problem drinkers, and alcoholics to help students identify problems with parental drinking and offers suggestions for seeking further information or help.

289. Bayle-Lissick, Sheila, and Elise M. Jahns. **Creating Choices: How Adult Children Can Turn Today's Dreams into Tomorrow's Reality.** Center City, MN: Hazelden, 1990. 249 pp.

   Designed to help adult children of alcoholics feel a sense of empowerment and control over their lives. Focuses on developing purpose and spirituality, setting realistic goals, fostering self-esteem, and learning to deal with problem situations. Suggests ways to create and take advantage of positive choices in life and describes a variety of activities to help change negative feelings and behavior patterns. Also includes a chapter describing possible situations that may confront ACOAs in the workplace and suggests ways to deal effectively with these. References, bibliography, index.

290. Beattie, Melody. **Beyond Codependency and Getting Better All the Time.** Center City, MN: Hazelden, 1989. 252 pp.

   Focuses on identifying compulsive and unhealthy coping mechanisms that may develop in dysfunctional family situations and suggests practical ways of replacing these with positive, healthy behaviors. There are case histories of spouses and adult children--many from alcoholic homes-- that illustrate how unhealthy reactions develop into established behavior patterns that may continue to surface after an alcoholic or codependent is recovering. Discusses the core issues of recovery, including relapse, dealing with shame, coming to terms with family of origin, and bolstering self-esteem. The section on relationships provides helpful insights into the need for setting personal boundaries and for avoiding potentially harmful associations. Each chapter concludes with suggested activities to help the reader explore related personal experiences and issues. An audiocassette adapted from the text is also available. Sequel to Codependent No More (item 291). References, bibliography.

291.    Beattie, Melody. **Codependent No More: How to Stop Controlling Others and Start Caring for Yourself.** Center City, MN: Hazelden, 1987. 229 pp.

Helps define codependence and offers practical suggestions for recovery from this disorder. Part one explores the evolution and various definitions of codependency and outlines the common characteristics. Part two focuses on "the basics of self-care" to help codependents learn how to separate themselves from their dependent and their disease and learn to rebuild their own lives. Chapters include suggested activities to help codependents relate the text to their own situations. References, bibliography.

292.    Becker, Robert. **Addicted to Misery: The Other Side of Co-Dependency.** Deerfield Beach, FL: Health Communications, 1989. 83 pp.

Discusses the problems adult children of alcoholics frequently have in maintaining healthy lifestyles, even after participation in recovery programs. Outlines symptoms of codependency that focus on denial of feelings, lack of trust, and worry, and demonstrates how these patterns evolve from childhood into adult life, leading to fear of change and expectation of catastrophe. Offers practical advice to help adult children identify "miserable thinking," remove the medicators that have served as enablers of this pattern, and begin the risk-taking behavior necessary for complete recovery. There is a lengthy appendix of self-help and information organizations. Bibliography.

293.    Benson, Mary E. **From Behind the Front: Shame, Abuse, Codependency and Addiction in Our Lives.** Dunedin, New Zealand: Chintillga Press, 1988. 71 pp.

Focuses on the development and consequences of shame resulting from family situations in which there was physical, sexual, or verbal abuse or addiction. Functions as a workbook to help adults understand and identify the effects of shame on their lives and advocates gender-specific counseling and support groups for most effective treatment. Includes a very helpful discussion of covert incest. Useful for adult children of alcoholics and therapists who work with them.

294.    Birke, Szifra, and Kathy Mayer. **Private Practice.** Denver: MAC Publishing, 1987. 352 pp.

Uses the setting of a fictional support group for adult children of alcoholics to describe some of the emotional and behavioral effects of growing up in an alcoholic home. Follows the progress of group members through their examinations of roles and behaviors related to family alcoholism, moving toward a goal of emotional freedom and recovery. The text is written specifically for ACOAs and offers readers the chance to participate in the fictional group by recording comments about group members as well as observations about personal feelings and issues. A short list of resources for further information is included. Bibliography.

295.    Black, Claudia. **It Will Never Happen to Me!** Denver: MAC Publishing, 1982. 183 pp.

Focuses attention on the effects of alcoholism on family members. Identifies family roles commonly assumed by children of alcoholics and discusses the effects of these childhood roles on adult life. Also suggests ways to identify and understand some negative adult behavior patterns. In addition, there is a chapter on family violence, both physical and sexual, and how to handle it. Especially helpful for spouses and adult children of alcoholics.

296.    Black, Claudia. **Repeat After Me.** Denver: MAC, 1985. 154 pp.

Offers step-by-step guidelines to help adults who were raised in alcoholic or other dysfunctional homes. The text consists of a series of writing exercises designed to explore past family relationships and resulting adult difficulties that may be experienced in expressing feelings, learning to trust and accept, relinquishing the need to control, and developing self-esteem. The exercises are intended as a self-help tool and may be completed at the individual's own pace. There is no suggested follow-up, resource list, or references.

297.    Bowden, Julie D., and Herbert L. Gravitz. **Genesis: Spirituality in Recovery from Childhood Traumas.** Deerfield Beach, FL: Health Communications, 1988. 111 pp.

Follow-up to earlier book **Recovery: A Guide for Adult Children of Alcoholics** (item 308). Describes in detail the final stage of recovery for adult children--genesis--which incorporates spiritual experience and understanding into a recovering lifestyle. Discusses the importance of genesis to recovery and explains the relationship to religion and to Alcoholics Anonymous. Offers suggestions for attaining genesis and cautions against several obstacles that may hinder its achievement. Written for ACOAs or other adult children of trauma. References.

298. Castine, Jacqueline. **Recovery from Rescuing.** Deerfield Beach, FL: Health Communications, 1989. 113 pp.

Offers practical suggestions to adult children of alcoholics, workaholics, health care professionals, and other codependents who suffer from a compulsion to sacrifice themselves to serve the needs of others. Uses an informal question-and-answer format to differentiate between rescuing and helping and between responsibility and over-responsibility. Includes a list of support groups for rescuers as well as several "step" programs to aid in personal recovery. Bibliography.

299. Cermak, Timmen L. **A Primer on Children of Alcoholics.** Deerfield Beach, FL: Health Communications, 1985. 52 pp.

Provides adult children of alcoholics with basic information about the disease of alcoholism and its effects on them and offers guidelines for recovery. Describes codependency and its manifestation in ACOAs, including its effects on family roles. Identifies the emotional and behavioral characteristics of ACOAs and discusses how these develop from childhood. Offers a five-stage model of recovery to help ACOAs break through their denial, work on underlying core issues, and establish new belief systems. Briefly discusses the treatment process and offers suggestions for selecting a therapist or type of treatment.

300. Cermak, Timmen L. **A Time to Heal: The Road to Recovery for Adult Children of Alcoholics.** Los Angeles: Jeremy P. Tarcher, 1988. 227 pp.

Focuses on the psychological and emotional problems experienced by adults who grew up with alcoholic parents and offers hope for recovery. Discusses the importance of breaking down denial to accept and understand the effects of childhood trauma--including an explanation of post-traumatic stress disorder as it is manifested in some ACOAs--and outlines a journey through five stages of recovery from survival to genesis (incorporating spirituality). There is a description of twelve-step programs as they relate to ACOA recovery, as well as a discussion of other treatment approaches and guidelines for selecting a therapist. Appendixes include practical advice for dealing with active alcoholic parents, brief supportive hints for friends and family concerned about ACOAs, information about the National Association for Children of Alcoholics, and a list of diagnostic criteria for co-dependence. Intended primarily for ACOAs and therapists who deal with them. Bibliography.

301.    Dean, Amy E. **Feeling Better: Nurturing Self-Esteem.** Center City, MN: Hazelden, 1988. 27 pp.

Discusses how an adult's self-esteem may have been adversely affected by growing up in a dysfunctional family (such as one in which parental alcoholism was present). Suggests ways to build a greater sense of self-worth through goal setting, risk taking, sharing feelings, developing better decision-making skills, and caring for one's physical and emotional well-being.

302.    Dean, Amy E. **Is This Program for Me? The Roots and Rights of the Recovering Adult Child.** Center City, MN: Hazelden, 1987. 19 pp.

Describes some of the common problems suffered by adults who grew up in homes with an alcoholic parent. Identifies five important needs (or rights) that an ACOA must satisfy in order to be free of the negative effects of the past and offers suggestions for meeting these needs through self-help groups such as Al-Anon. Includes a helpful summary of the goals and rewards of recovery.

303.    Dean, Amy E. **Making Changes: How Adult Children Can Have Healthier, Happier Relationships.** Center City, MN: Hazelden, 1988. 72 pp.

Helps adult children of alcoholics understand how present unhealthy relationships may be based on past relationships to alcoholic parents. Part one focuses on understanding the differences between healthy and unhealthy relationships. There is a separate chapter that demonstrates how childhood roles and responses to the dysfunctional family situation can lead to particular unhealthy adult behavior patterns. In part two guidelines are presented to help ACOAs make positive changes in their relationships in five specific areas: trust, honesty, individuality, nurturing, and knowledge. There is also discussion of a twelve-step program, based on Alcoholics Anonymous, that is recommended as a tool for improving relationships. Includes suggested writing activities for self-assessment of behaviors.

304.    Dean, Amy E. **Once Upon a Time.** Center City, MN: Hazelden, 1987. 165 pp.

Recounts the personal stories of twenty adults who grew up in alcoholic or other dysfunctional families. Each story describes the problems experienced in childhood and shows how they led to unhealthy relationships and behavior patterns--including alcohol and drug abuse--in adult life. There is also discussion of how each person began the road to recovery with the help of Al-Anon, Alcoholics Anonymous, or special ACOA support groups. However, a list of such organizations with addresses is not included.

305.    Earll, Bob. **I Got Tired of Pretending.** Tucson, AZ: STEM Publications, 1988. 110 pp.

Describes the author's personal experiences growing up in an alcoholic home and the emotional and behavioral effects on his adult life. Discusses the importance of discovering one's "inner child" in order to fully understand and accept the painful experiences related to family alcoholism and suggests a path toward forgiveness and freedom from the past. Bibliography.

306.    Friends in Recovery. **The Twelve Steps--A Way Out:
        A Working Guide for Adult Children of Alcoholics
        and Other Dysfunctional Families.** San Diego:
        Recovery Publications, 1987. 195 pp.

        Designed to help adult children of alcoholics work
through (in writing and discussion) their feelings about
growing up in an alcoholic home. The text is prepared in
workbook format, with questions and explanations based on
a twelve-step program adapted from Alcoholics Anonymous.
May be used for individual study or with "step study"
workshops utilizing small groups to simulate healthy family
communications. Appendixes contain guidelines for
individual and group study, detailed instructions for
conducting step study workshops, and discussion questions
for workshop participants. May also be used with **The
Twelve Steps for Adult Children\*** of Alcoholic and Other
**Dysfunctional Families** (item 307), which provides a more
detailed explanation of each of the steps.

307.    Friends in Recovery. **The Twelve Steps for Adult
        Children\* of Alcoholics and Other Dysfunctional
        Families.** San Diego: Recovery Publications, 1987.
        93 pp.

        Describes a twelve-step program based on Alcoholics
Anonymous that can help adult children of alcoholics
understand and express their feelings about an unhealthy
childhood and develop a sense of self-worth to cope with
present situations. Based on a spiritual, rather than
intellectual, approach toward alcoholism that requires a
belief in some type of higher power. Appendixes include a
list of self-help organizations, a brief reading list, the
Twelve Steps of Alcoholics Anonymous, and a daily
meditation. May be used as part of a writing step study
workshop in conjunction with **The Twelve Steps--A Way
Out** (item 306).

308.    Gravitz, Herbert L., and Julie D. Bowden. **Recovery:
        A Guide for Adult Children of Alcoholics.** New
        York: Fireside/Learning Publication, 1987. 120 pp.

        Written to help adult children of alcoholics
understand and deal with the personal suffering that
resulted from growing up with an alcoholic parent. In the
first three chapters the book examines the roots of the
emotional and psychological damage inflicted by an
alcoholic family system as well as the coping skills of
denial and repression most frequently used to survive in
this unhealthy family atmosphere. The remaining chapters
provide guidance to move ACOAs from the stage of
acceptance through confrontation of core issues, such as
personal control, trust, and intimacy, toward an ultimate
goal of spiritual and emotional well-being. There is a short
reading list of books and a list of organizations for further
information. Although the book is intended primarily for
the lay public, the authors do cite the work of a number
of other alcohol professionals and researchers. An earlier
edition (1985) was titled **Guide to Recovery: A Book for
Adult Children of Alcoholics.** References, index.

309.    Hobe, Phyllis. **Lovebound: Recovering from an
        Alcoholic Family.** New York: NAL Books, 1990.
        241 pp.

        Offers a different view of recovery for adult
children of alcoholics that challenges the prevailing twelve-
step approach of most ACOA support groups. Argues that
the traditional A.A.-style approach, which may be effective
for alcoholics, only serves to keep adult children in a
repetitive pattern of self-destructive behavior based on
feelings of powerlessness, guilt, and denial of legitimate
anger. Questions the ability of alcoholics to truly love
their children while preoccupied with their disease and
suggests that true recovery for ACOAs must be preceded
by this awareness. Recommends a path toward recovery
that involves the release of buried anger, forgiveness, and
development of self-regard.

310.    Koons, Carolyn. **Beyond Betrayal: Healing My Broken Past.** New York: Harper and Row, 1986. 275 pp.

Relates the true story of the author's stormy childhood with two alcoholic parents. Describes the physical and verbal abuse, as well as neglect, that usually accompanied heavy drinking episodes by one or both parents. Illustrates how this unhealthy domestic environment led to the author's delinquent behavior and heavy drinking. The second half of the text focuses on her involvement with a Christian youth fellowship, which helped her journey away from the past toward a new lifestyle and career in youth fellowship and education. Appropriate for adult children or older teens as well as counselors and clergy who deal with troubled families.

311.    Kritsberg, Wayne. **The Adult Children of Alcoholics Syndrome: From Discovery to Recovery.** Deerfield Beach, FL: Health Communications, 1985. 150 pp.

Describes the physical and emotional problems most frequently manifested in adults who grew up in alcoholic families and offers a recovery system designed to promote a more healthy lifestyle. Part one of the text defines four types of alcoholic families and describes the survival roles and rules that nonalcoholic members adopt. The emotional, mental, physical, and behavioral characteristics of ACOAs are outlined, and there is a description of how family trauma may result in chronic shock for COAs who are unable to deal with the emotional effects of severe family disturbances. In part two the author introduces his Family Integration System--a recovery process designed to help ACOAs discharge repressed emotions and develop positive thinking and life skills. He describes in detail the activities involved in this system, which may be incorporated in a variety of treatment settings. The book is written for ACOAs or therapists.

312.    Kritsberg, Wayne. **Healing Together: A Guide to Intimacy and Recovery for Co-Dependent Couples.** Deerfield Beach, FL: Health Communications, 1990. 132 pp.

Focuses on the difficulties with intimate relationships that may be experienced by adult children from alcoholic or other dysfunctional families. Presumes that all persons from dysfunctional families become codependent--i.e., emotionally dependent on an outside source to build feelings of self-esteem. Discusses how codependence can affect adult sexual and emotional relationships, including a chapter on the special problems of sexual abuse survivors. Offers practical advice and simple exercises to help couples improve communication and strengthen their physical and emotional relationships. Written for couples in which one or both members are adult children. Bibliography.

313.    Larsen, Earnie. **Old Patterns, New Truths: Beyond the Adult Child Syndrome.** Center City, MN: Hazelden, 1988. 104 pp.

Written in workbook format to help adult children deal with the emotional and behavioral consequences of growing up in alcoholic or other dysfunctional homes. Recovery exercises are based on identifying unhealthy reaction patterns and replacing them with a more effective support system and positive life skills. Each chapter ends with a writing activity that is designed to help expose negative behaviors or to identify strengths to aid in building self-esteem. Could be used in ACOA support groups.

314.    McConnell, Patty. **A Workbook for Healing Adult Children of Alcoholics.** San Francisco: Harper and Row, 1986. 170 pp.

Contains exercises to help adult children of alcoholics understand and cope with the results of growing up with an alcoholic parent. Part one focuses on accepting and understanding the emotional harm inflicted in an alcoholic home. Exercises cover childhood experiences as well as adult feelings and behaviors. Part two presents activities to enhance emotional recovery through forgiveness, self-knowledge, and positive expression of feelings. Bibliography.

315.      Marlin, Emily. **Hope: New Choices and Recovery Strategies for Adult Children of Alcoholics.** New York: Harper and Row, 1987. 287 pp.

Offers guidelines to help adult children of alcoholics move beyond survival toward greater personal fulfillment. In part one readers are helped to reexamine their experiences of growing up in an alcoholic home in order to better understand the effects on their adult lives. Part two focuses on the process of change. There are chapters on various types of support groups and therapeutic approaches to help in the recovery process. There are also discussions of key issues in recovery, such as mourning past losses, forgiveness, the need to control, building self-esteem, and establishing trust. Part three deals with rebuilding relationships with parents and siblings and includes a section on interventions to motivate drinking parents into treatment. There are seven helpful self-tests on family alcoholism and its effects as well as brief descriptions of organizations that provide information and referral services appropriate for children of alcoholics.

316.      Martin, Sara H. **Healing for Adult Children of Alcoholics.** Nashville, TN: Broadman Press, 1988. 191 pp.

Provides a good overview of the problems experienced by adults who have grown up in alcoholic homes. Describes the various roles and communication styles that are used by children and nonalcoholic spouses to cope within a dysfunctional family system and discusses the impact of such behaviors on children's physical and emotional development. Separate chapters focus on the marital styles, parenting styles, and work styles of ACOAs, all of which may be negatively affected by childhood trauma. Presents guidelines for overcoming the effects of the past and for developing healthy relationships, along with suggestions for learning to deal with sober or drinking alcoholic parents. There is also a chapter on the spiritual life of ACOAs which examines how children's understanding and relationship with God may be affected by an alcoholic home situation. Bibliography.

317. Mellody, Pia, Andrea W. Miller, and J. Keith Miller. **Facing Codependence: What It Is, Where It Comes From, How It Sabotages Our Lives.** New York: Harper and Row, 1989. 222 pp.

Presents an in-depth discussion of the phenomenon of codependence, focusing on how it develops and the effects it has on adult behaviors and relationships. Examines the basic nature of the child as it is influenced by growing up in a functional or dysfunctional home and looks at the various types of parental abuse that may produce codependent adults. Concludes with a brief chapter of suggestions for initiating personal recovery from codependency. Although the book does not deal exclusively with alcoholic families, parental alcoholism is one of a variety of dysfunctional behaviors that are identified as contributing factors in abuse and codependence. The appendix contains a very good brief history of codependence, citing its roots in the study of alcoholic families. Useful for therapists and recovering adults. References, index.

318. Middelton-Moz, Jane, and Lorie Dwinell. **After the Tears: Reclaiming the Personal Losses of Childhood.** Deerfield Beach, FL: Health Communications, 1986. 141 pp.

Helps adult children of alcoholics deal with emotional aftereffects of growing up in a dysfunctional family environment. Focuses particularly on the ACOA's inability to deal with the loss of a normal, loving, and consistent parental relationship. The authors advocate griefwork to help ACOAs understand and accept this loss in order to free themselves to experience feelings, choices, and healthy relationships. Uses several case histories to illustrate the trauma suffered by ACOAs in childhood and the effects on adult behaviors. Also presents a juxtaposition of a normal and an alcoholic family situation to demonstrate the dysfunction in the alcoholic home. This well-written text is intended for ACOAs, their families, and the professionals that deal with them. Bibliography.

319.    Miller, Joy. **Addictive Relationships: Reclaiming Your Boundaries.** Deerfield Beach, FL: Health Communications, 1989. 108 pp.

Offers help for adult children from alcoholic families who are experiencing difficulties with interpersonal relationships. Uses short case histories to illustrate how dysfunctional family patterns from childhood can lead to later problems such as manipulation, caretaking, lack of trust, and fear of being alone. Suggests practical steps for improving relationships by establishing "boundaries" to protect and enhance self-worth. Includes worksheets to record daily progress toward personal goals and to identify and resolve feelings of shame rooted in current or past experiences. Bibliography.

320.    Miller, Joy, and Marianne Ripper. **Following the Yellow Brick Road: The Adult Child's Personal Journey Through Oz.** Deerfield Beach, FL: Health Communications, 1988. 192 pp.

Uses the analogy of Dorothy's journey through Oz to serve as a guideline for adult children who are recovering from the trauma of growing up in an alcoholic home. Identifies six stages through which ACOAs must travel in their journey toward recovery: isolation, denial, anger, bargaining, depression, and acceptance. Uses characters from the Oz story to describe the roles that may be played by children in alcoholic homes. There is a "progression and recovery chart" for each role to help illustrate the changes through which the recovering adult must work. There is also a chapter to help ACOAs understand and cope successfully with relapse symptoms. The book is primarily addressed to ACOAs rather than therapists and deals only briefly with treatment strategies. Bibliography.

321.    Oliver-Diaz, Philip, and Patricia A. O'Gorman. **Twelve Steps to Self-Parenting for Adult Children of Alcoholics.** Deerfield Beach, FL: Health Communications, 1988. 135 pp.

Provides direction for adult children of alcoholics who want to overcome the emotional and behavioral consequences of their dysfunctional childhoods. Uses the concepts of "inner child" and "higher parent" to describe respectively the individual's feelings and spontaneity as opposed to inner wisdom and intuitive knowledge, all of which are seen as necessary for healthy functioning. The text is divided into twelve chapters corresponding to the Twelve Steps of Alcoholics Anonymous. For each chapter a self-parenting step is described to help ACOAs deal with issues resulting from their own experiences of family alcoholism--lack of trust, fear of intimacy, shame, low self-esteem. Each chapter concludes with meditations and daily affirmations for reinforcing positive feelings and behaviors. May be used individually or with ACOA groups.

322.    Ray, Veronica. **A Design for Growth: How the Twelve Steps Work for Adult Children.** Center City, MN: Hazelden, 1988. 112 pp.

Describes how the Twelve Steps of the Al-Anon and Alcoholics Anonymous programs can be used as recovery tools by adult children of alcoholics. Each step is discussed in a separate chapter with a personal story to illustrate its effect on ACOAs. There is lengthy discussion of the belief in a higher power as the foundation for successfully working the Twelve Steps. Appendixes contain a brief list of organizations for further help, a reading list, and suggested affirmations and techniques for meditation. Bibliography, index.

323.    Robinson, Bryan E. **Work Addiction: Hidden Legacies of Adult Children.** Deerfield Beach, FL: Health Communications, 1989. 179 pp.

Examines the phenomenon of compulsive overworking that is often manifested by adults who grew up in alcoholic or dysfunctional homes. Identifies common physical and behavioral signs of work addiction and demonstrates how these patterns may evolve from childhood survival skills to adult work patterns. Offers practical suggestions to help break the cycle of work addiction. Includes instruments to help measure degree of work addiction, type A and B behavior patterns in children (as a potential factor in developing work addiction), and life balance between healthy work, family, play, and self. Useful for workers as well as employers to increase awareness of problems on the job caused by work addiction. Contains an annotated bibliography of books, periodicals, newsletters, magazines, and organizations related to children and adult children of alcoholics, stress, and work addiction.

324.    Rosellini, Gayle, and Mark Worden. **Taming Your Turbulent Past: A Self-Help Guide for Adult Children.** Deerfield Beach, FL: Health Communications, 1987. 183 pp.

Written as a practical guide to help adult children from alcoholic families learn to develop their own healthy lifestyles free of their childhood trauma. Examines the negative influence of hidden anger and resentment toward the past on present behavior and feelings. Offers several suggestions and exercises to help release resentment and cope with stress. Also explores special issues such as nutritional problems, risk of chemical dependency, and building self-esteem.

325.     Schlesinger, Stephen E., and John J. Gillick. **Stop Drinking and Start Living.** 2d ed. Blue Ridge Summit, PA: TAB Books, 1989. 181 pp.

Provides practical advice to help alcoholics and their families find help for alcohol-related problems. Part one presents basic information on alcohol, its effects on the body, and the disease of alcoholism. Part two offers suggestions for problem drinkers who want to get help. In part three guidelines are provided to help family members cope with an alcoholic and get help for themselves. There is a separate chapter on adult children of alcoholics that describes family characteristics as well as attitudes and character traits of ACOAs. There is also a brief review of research on the resilient characteristics of COAs that may protect them (as children and adults) against the negative impact of an alcoholic family. Appendixes include lists of resource organizations for further help, state and regional alcoholism programs, and state highway safety offices. This book would be useful for all adult members (and older teens) in an alcoholic family. Index.

326.     Seixas, Judith S., and Geraldine Youcha. **Children of Alcoholism: A Survivor's Manual.** New York: Crown Publishers, 1985. 208 pp.

Uses case histories to describe the experiences and feelings common to many children who grew up in alcoholic homes and discusses the effects of these experiences on adult lifestyles and relationships. Offers sensitive and practical advice for coping with these effects of alcoholism and for dealing with other family members, including children and alcoholic parents. Contains resources for further information and help. Bibliography, index.

327.    W., Kathleen. **Healing a Broken Heart: Twelve Steps of Recovery for Adult Children.** Deerfield Beach, FL: Health Communications, 1988. 95 pp.

Describes a twelve-step program, based on Alcoholics Anonymous, to help adults recover from the psychological and emotional consequences of growing up with alcoholic parents. Defines the goals of the program as helping ACOAs to work through feelings of isolation, fear, and anger and to develop healthy self-parenting skills. The author uses her own experiences to illustrate how each step has helped her recovery, and she offers some very brief suggestions to help others adapt the steps to their situations. The book is intended to stimulate discussion in ACOA self-help groups.

328.    W., Kathleen, and Jewell E. **With Gentleness, Humor and Love: A 12-Step Guide for Adult Children in Recovery.** Deerfield Beach, FL: Health Communications, 1989. 105 pp.

Designed as a workbook to help adult children of alcoholics move through a twelve-step recovery program. The text is intended to serve as a link between traditional twelve-step literature and workshop-oriented therapies. The authors present three tools--victim roles and freedom wheels, guided visualization/active imagination, and creative action routines--and suggest ways that these tools can be used to work through specific recovery steps. These suggested practices are intended to be flexible for individual or group work. The focus of the tools and exercises is on honesty, acceptance, and "reparenting" one's inner child, whose true identity was unable to evolve in a dysfunctional family.

329.  Wegscheider-Cruse, Sharon. **The Miracle: Healing for Adult Children and Co-Dependents.** Rapid City, SD: Nurturing Networks, 1987. 42 pp.

Outlines a four-step process to help adult children of alcoholics develop positive attitudes toward life and self and healthy relationships with others. The steps involve reframing thinking to release denial of painful experiences from the past, learning to welcome and express feelings (both good and bad), choosing risk and change in order to break free of unhealthy lifestyles, and nurturing self to reinforce positive changes in behavior and attitudes. Illustrations.

330.  Wegscheider-Cruse, Sharon. **The Miracle of Recovery: Healing for Addicts, Adult Children and Co-Dependents.** Deerfield Beach, FL: Health Communications, 1989. 217 pp.

Offers practical suggestions for recovering from codependency--defined as preoccupation with and dependency on another person, substance, or behavior. Much of the book focuses on the author's own story of growing up with alcoholic parents and her personal and professional involvement in family alcoholism issues. Her guidelines for recovery center on the ability to make positive choices and to develop self-worth. There are a number of short chapters dealing with issues such as workaholism, divorce, and step-parenting. However, many of these chapters are too brief (1-2 pages) to be more than outlines or anecdotes, and they cause the text to be somewhat choppy. The final section is a compilation of personal stories by codependents. Appropriate for adult children of alcoholics and for counselors or leaders of self-help groups that deal with family issues.

331.  Whitfield, Charles L. **A Gift to Myself: A Personal Workbook and Guide to Healing My Child Within.** Deerfield Beach, FL: Health Communications, 1990. 260 pp.

Presents exercises to help adult children recover from the effects of growing up in an alcoholic or other dysfunctional family. The exercises are designed to rediscover one's "child within" (or true inner self) by identifying feelings and needs, by grieving the losses and traumas of the past, and by working through core issues of the dynamics of codependence. Describes the stages in the recovery process and offers suggestions to help ACOAs select a support group or therapist for additional help. Appendixes include a sample form for exploring problems in one's family of origin and a family drinking survey. May be used as a workbook to accompany **Healing the Child Within** (item 332). Bibliography.

332. Whitfield, Charles L. **Healing the Child Within: Discovery and Recovery for Adult Children of Dysfunctional Families.** Deerfield Beach, FL: Health Communications, 1987. 152 pp.

Written for adults who were exposed to acute or prolonged childhood traumas, such as parental alcoholism, physical or sexual abuse, or chronic illness of a family member. Focuses on the recovery of the child within--the individual's true inner feelings, desires, creativity, and spontaneity. Discusses how a dysfunctional family situation leads to the development of a codependent self that inhibits the free expression of feelings. Offers detailed guidelines for learning to accept and to handle repressed emotions and for restoring and nurturing the inner self. Includes several helpful charts, tables, and questionnaires to aid in self-assessment. References.

333. Wholey, Dennis. **Becoming Your Own Parent: The Solution for Adult Children of Alcoholic and Other Dysfunctional Families.** New York: Doubleday, 1988. 285 pp.

Relates personal experiences of fourteen persons who were raised in dysfunctional homes. Offers the guidance of several well-known experts on adult children for identifying and coping with the effects of unresolved childhood issues. The first part of the text contains the personal stories, which range from parental alcoholism to physical abuse and workaholism. Part two presents discussions by experts of some of the major problems associated with dysfunctional families: low self-worth, poor survival skills, negative characteristics, compulsions and addictions, codependency, addictive relationships, and intimacy. In part three experts offer solutions for resolving old issues and working toward a healthy, recovering lifestyle. This could serve as introductory reading for ACOAs and therapists who have no background in this area. It does not deal with specific treatment approaches.

334.    Woititz, Janet G. **Guidelines for Support Groups: Adult Children of Alcoholics and Others Who Identify.** Deerfield Beach, FL: Health Communications, 1986. 37 pp.

Discusses the importance and goals of self-help groups for adult children of alcoholics and outlines a format for meetings based on the Twelve Steps of Alcoholics Anonymous and Al-Anon. Includes a detailed guide for conducting a Step Four inventory to identify negative characteristics, such as self-pity and jealousy, and suggests a seven-step process to work towards positive change. The text is written for ACOAs who wish to organize or increase the effectiveness of support groups. Attendance in A.A. or Al-Anon or knowledge of the Twelve Steps is recommended.

335.    Wolter, Dwight L. **Forgiving Our Parents: For Adult Children from Dysfunctional Families.** Minneapolis: CompCare, 1989. 86 pp.

Discusses the importance of forgiveness to help adult children come to terms with the effects of parental dysfunction. The author uses experiences and feelings from his childhood with a violent, alcoholic father to illustrate how true forgiveness is based on understanding and acceptance of parental behavior. He also discusses the role of self-forgiveness as a necessary prerequisite for recovery from childhood trauma and for successful parenting of future children.

## Journal Articles

336.    Frye, David E. "Griefwork and the Adult Children of Alcoholic Families." *COA Review* No. 10 & 11(1986): 8-12.

Discusses the types of loss--material, physical, emotional--that adult children of alcoholics have often suffered from growing up in alcoholic families. Argues that adult children are often trapped in feelings and behavior patterns that are rigid, controlling, and self-destructive because they never accepted and mourned the losses of their childhood. Describes the process of griefwork as necessary to help ACOAs stop blaming their parents and start rebuilding their own lives. References.

337.    Gunning, Paul. "Alcoholic ACOAs: Insights to Erickson, Ego Growth and the 12-Steps of AA." *Focus on Chemically Dependent Families* 10(Jan.-Feb. 1987): 20-21, 26-27.

Explains why alcoholics may have additional problems in recovery if they are also children of alcoholics. Suggests that parental alcoholism may seriously interfere with childhood development and that personality restructuring for ACOAs may be necessary for successful recovery. Uses Erickson's stages of human development to illustrate how the Alcoholics Anonymous program can be used as a tool for building a healthy ego while achieving sobriety.

338.    Hunter, Mic. "Healing Shame and Guilt: Paradox of
        the 12-Step Process for ACoAs." *Focus on
        Chemically Dependent Families* 11(Feb.-Mar. 1988):
        26, 29-31.

        Describes shame as the major problem underlying
the feelings and behaviors of adult children of alcoholics.
Differentiates shame--a feeling of low self-worth--from
guilt, which the author defines as an appropriate response
for deviating from one's value system. Outlines a twelve-
step process for ACOAs which is designed to change
shame-based behavior to guilt-based behavior.

339.    Johnson, Jan. "Creating Healthy Rituals for You and
        Your Family." *Changes* 4(May-June 1989): 36-37.

        Discusses the role of family rituals in promoting
healthy family relationships and preventing substance abuse
and offers practical suggestions to help adult children of
alcoholics establish rituals in their own families. Covers
family celebrations, holidays, and vacations as well as
personal time and planned interactions with family members
and friends.

340.    Krill, Phil. "ACOAs: Addiction to Addiction." *The
        Counselor* 7(Nov.-Dec. 1989): 24-25.

        Discusses why adult children of alcoholics are
frequently attracted to the helping professions and
illustrates how they may become addicted to the field of
addiction itself. Differentiates between the use of insight
(special knowledge which may be supplemented with the aid
of recovery resources) and actual involvement with
recovering clients and argues that action is the essential
ingredient for recovery of professionals and lay persons.

341.    O'Gorman, Patricia. "The Art of Self-Parenting:
        How to Get Free of Compulsive Family Secrets."
        *Focus on Chemically Dependent Families* 11(Apr.-
        May 1988): 22-23, 38.

Uses the concepts of "inner child" and "higher parent" to describe the individual's creative, spontaneous self, which is protected by the objective, problem-solving self. The author discusses how adult children of alcoholics, as a result of family trauma, may have been deprived as children of the wisdom of their higher parent and may have suppressed the feelings of the inner child. When such coping patterns continue into adulthood, the individual may be characterized by compulsive dependency and a strong need for control. The author advocates a self-parenting approach to help ACOAs reach self-forgiveness and acceptance and learn to live in the present.

342.   Wilson, C.C. "ACA Comes of Age." *Changes* 4(May-June 1989): 24, 54-56.

Describes the beginnings of the twelve-step groups for adult children of alcoholics. Discusses how and why many of these groups have separated from Al-Anon and examines their growth and focus.

See also: 79, 148, 150-51, 182, 200, 204-5, 208, 211, 213-16, 220, 222, 226, 228-29, 231-32, 243, 246-47, 251, 279.

## 11. FICTION

### Books and Pamphlets

The entries in this chapter describe novels written for adults and mature teens about the experiences of growing up in an alcoholic family. Fiction for younger teens and pre-teens is covered in chapter 6, **Children: Fiction.**

343.     Ellis, Dan C. **Legacies of an Alcoholic Family.** Deerfield Beach, FL: Health Communications, 1988. 140 pp.

Describes three generations of alcoholism in one family. Interweaves the stories of Sam Bruner, his son John, and John's son Bobby to show the common threads as well as differences in their lifestyles, coping skills, and substance abuse. The dialog seems contrived to prove a point, which makes the book read more like a therapist's case history than a novel. Also, the author only skims the surface in describing the roles and reactions of other family members, particularly siblings. Could be used as background reading for adults or older teens who are beginning their recovery.

344.     Glynn, Thomas. **Watching the Body Burn.** New York: Alfred A. Knopf, 1989. 300 pp.

Powerful fictional account of a young man's memories of growing up with an alcoholic father. The story unfolds not as a cohesive chronological tale but rather as a series of images, often juxtaposed, that vividly capture the bizarre environment of an alcoholic home. This is a gripping and sometimes brutal testament to the emotional ravaging that can follow children of alcoholics into adulthood. Not recommended for high-school ages or younger.

345.    Heckler, Jonellen. **A Fragile Peace.** New York: G.P. Putnam's Sons, 1986. 300 pp.

Novel about the daily experiences of a family suffering from alcoholism. Illustrates the crippling effects of denial as practiced by the alcoholic father and his well-intentioned enabling wife. Also demonstrates how the teenage son and daughter are drawn into the need to preserve "a fragile peace" within their family. The devastating emotional and financial impact on the entire family is described in terms of lost opportunities-- friendships, jobs, college, and family ties. This is a candid, moving account of alcoholism as a family disease; it provides an excellent depiction of the roles of enabler, hero, and scapegoat. Suitable for older teens and adults.

346.    McFarland, Dennis. **The Music Room.** Boston: Houghton Mifflin, 1990. 275 pp.

Compelling story centered around a young man's search to discover the reason for his brother's suicide and for his own apparent failures. With an unusual technique that blends flashbacks with present experiences and premonitions of the future, the author paints a troubled portrait of a man raised by two wealthy alcoholic parents-- a father who was a failed musician and drank himself to death and a mother who was an ex-showgirl and continues to drink in the family mansion. The narrator, whose wife has just left him for another man, is stunned by the death of his brother, a successful composer who had shown no negative effects from his family background. As he endeavors to find the truth, Martin begins to understand his brother's pain as well as his own. He also begins to understand his mother's inner strength and to separate this from her failures as a parent. This is a beautifully written story of alcoholism and family relationships that is imaginative, realistic, and optimistic.

347.   Winthrop, Elizabeth. **In My Mother's House.** New York: Doubleday, 1988. 523 pp.

Tells a story of incest and alcoholism that affects the lives of three generations of women. Depicts candidly the actions and emotions of a young girl who is molested by her alcoholic uncle and demonstrates how this trauma later inhibits her relationship with her husband and her daughter. The daughter's unhappy marriage to an alcoholic and her emotional sterility create a gulf between herself and her own daughter. Not until after the grandmother's death and the revelation of her childhood experiences are mother and daughter able to understand and accept their own past and their feelings for each other. This is an absorbing account of the multi-generational effects of alcoholism on the family.

See also: 157, 164, 168, 294.

# APPENDIX A

## Resource Organizations

The organizations described below include self-help groups, professional associations, research institutes, and information centers that can be of help to children of alcoholics. Not all of these groups have services specifically for, or limited to, COAs, but all provide some type of service or information materials that would be helpful to family members of alcoholics in dealing with problems resulting from growing up with an alcoholic parent.

**Addiction Research Foundation (ARF),** 33 Russell St., Toronto, Ontario M5S 2S1, Canada, (416) 595-6100. Conducts research on alcoholism and other addictions and offers training programs for professionals in the alcohol and drug field. Publishes a variety of research and educational materials covering all aspects of alcoholism and drug abuse, including the effects on family members.

**Adult Children Educational Foundation (ACEF),** P.O. Box 454, McLean, VA 22101, (703) 356-6064 or (703) 821-2925 (bulletin board). Operates an electronic bulletin board with information for and about adult children and recovery issues. The bulletin board has over 70 files that can be accessed and downloaded by personal computer; files include information on self-help groups, lists of ACOA meetings, reviews of books and audiovisual materials, and a calendar of upcoming events of interest to ACOAs and professionals. Also publishes a newsletter and offers seminars and workshops for professionals and laypersons.

**Adult Children of Alcoholics (ACoA),** Interim World Service Organization, 2522 West Sepulveda Blvd., Suite 200, P.O. Box 3216, Torrance, CA 90505, (213) 534-1815. Promotes a twelve-step recovery program for adults who were raised in families where addiction was present. Supports the establishment of local ACOA self-help groups. Annual conference.

**Al-Anon/Alateen Family Group Headquarters,** P.O. Box 862, Midtown Station, New York, NY 10018-0862, (212) 302-7240 or (800) 356-9996. Offers self-help groups for family members of alcoholics. Al-Anon (for adults) and Alateen (for teenagers) follow the basic twelve-step structure of Alcoholics Anonymous (though they are separate fellowships). Although some Al-Anon groups have been formed primarily for adult children, they are not affiliated with other ACOA groups. Publications catalog, annual conference.

**Alcoholics Anonymous (AA),** A.A. World Services, Inc., Box 459, Grand Central Station, New York, NY 10163, (212) 686-1100. International fellowship of persons who feel they are suffering from a drinking problem. Provides mutual support and recovery from the disease of alcoholism through a program of Twelve Steps and Twelve Traditions. Publications catalog, annual conference.

**American Association for Protecting Children,** a division of the American Humane Association, 9725 East Hampden Ave., Denver, CO, 80231-4919, (303) 695-0811. Offers training and information for professionals regarding child abuse and neglect. Also serves as an advocate on the local and national levels for a safe environment for children.

Provides referral to appropriate resources for children and adult children of alcoholics. Publications catalog.

**Black Children of Alcoholic and Drug Addicted Persons (B/COADAP),** c/o Dr. Frances Larry Brisbane, 139 La Bonne Vie Dr. West, East Patchogue, NY 11720, (516) 654-2378 or (516) 444-3168. Self-help organization specifically for African Americans who grew up with an addicted parent.

**Children Are People, Too,** 493 Selby Ave., St. Paul, MN 55102, (612) 227-4031. Prevention program that includes a curriculum, supporting materials, and training for educators and counselors working with children in grades K-6. In addition to the chemical abuse curriculum model, this program also offers support group training for service providers who work with children from alcoholic or other dysfunctional families. Publications catalog.

**Children of Alcoholics Foundation, Inc.,** 200 Park Ave., 31st floor, New York, NY 10166, (212) 351-2680. Nonprofit organization that conducts research and offers publications on the problems and needs of children of alcoholics. Provides information and referral for children and adult children of alcoholics and has developed educational and professional curricula as well as audiovisual materials dealing specifically with children of alcoholics. Publications catalog.

**Community Intervention, Inc.,** 529 South Seventh St., Suite 570, Minneapolis, MN 55415, (612) 332-6537 or (800) 328-0417. Provides training, consultation services, and publications for professionals dealing with youth, alcohol, and drug issues. Also distributes materials for parents and youth, including children of alcoholics. Publications catalog.

**Families Anonymous (FA),** P.O. Box 528, Van Nuys, CA 91408, (818) 989-7841. Self-help organization for family members or friends who are concerned about a loved one's alcohol or other drug use. Offers a twelve-step program to help families understand and cope with the substance abuse problem. Publications catalog.

**Families in Action,** Drug Information Center, 3845 North Druid Hills Rd., Suite 300, Decatur, GA 30033, (404) 325-5799. Provides information to parents, educators, and others concerned with alcohol and other drug use among youth. Publications catalog.

**Nar-Anon Family Groups, Inc.,** World Service Office, P.O. Box 2562, Palos Verdes Peninsula, CA 90274, (213) 547-5800. Self-help groups for family members of persons who are abusing mood-altering drugs. Includes Narateen groups for teenagers and Preteen Nar-Anon for younger children. Companion, but separate, program to Narcotics Anonymous (see below).

**Narcotics Anonymous (NA),** World Service Office, P.O. Box 9999, Van Nuys, CA 91409, (818) 780-3951. Self-help fellowship for drug abusers. Offers a twelve-step recovery program based on the principles of Alcoholics Anonymous. Publications catalog.

**National Association for Children of Alcoholics (NACoA),** 31582 Coast Highway, Suite B, South Laguna, CA 92677, (714) 499-3889. Nonprofit organization that provides information and publications related to the needs and problems of children and adult children of alcoholics. State chapters were formed in 1987. Publications catalog, newsletter, annual conference.

**National Association for Native American Children of Alcoholics (NANACoA),** P.O. Box 3364, Seattle, WA 98114, (206) 324-9360. Serves as an information network and clearinghouse for Native American children of alcoholics. Provides training and support for Native American communities regarding the needs and services for COAs.

**National Black Alcoholism Council, Inc. (NBAC),** 53 West Jackson Blvd., Suite 828, Chicago, IL 60604, (312) 663-5780. Nonprofit organization of Black persons who are concerned about alcoholism and other drug abuse. Supports activities that promote development of, and access to, effective treatment and prevention services for Blacks. Offers counselor training, information services, and publications for children and adult children of alcoholics. State and local affiliates are available.

**National Clearinghouse for Alcohol and Drug Information (NCADI),** P.O. Box 2345, Rockville, MD 20852, (301) 468-2600 or (800) 729-6686. Provides information and materials on all aspects of alcohol and other drug use. Includes many materials designed for high-risk groups such as minorities and children of alcoholics. Publications catalog.

**National Council on Alcoholism and Drug Dependence (NCADD),** 12 West 21st St., New York, NY 10010, (212) 206-6770. Nonprofit organization providing public information, referral services, and publications about the prevention and treatment of alcohol and other drug problems, including the effects on family members. Offers a network of over 200 state and local affiliates. Publications catalog, annual conference.

**Rutgers University Center of Alcohol Studies (RUCAS),** Smithers Hall, Busch Campus, P.O. Box 969, Piscataway, NJ 08855-0969, (908) 932-4442 or (908) 932-2190. Conducts research and professional education on all aspects of alcohol use and problems. Offers clinical services to alcoholics and family members and provides information and materials to researchers and professionals in the alcohol and drug field. Includes information and publications on children of alcoholics. Publications catalog.

**Wisconsin Clearinghouse,** P.O. Box 1468, Madison, WI 53701-1468, (608) 263-2797 or (800) 262-6243. Provides information services and materials for parents, students, educators, and communities to prevent alcohol and drug problems. Includes materials for and about children of alcoholics. Publications catalog.

# APPENDIX B

## Audiovisual Resources

Prepared by Valerie Mead, M.L.S.
New Jersey Alcohol/Drug Resource Center and
Clearinghouse

Alcohol and other drug audiovisual materials have become more popular and more abundant in the past decade. These materials, which include films, video and audio cassettes, have not always received the same level of attention as print materials. While more journals and other reviewing sources are now including alcohol/drug film evaluations, the literature is still scarce and is found primarily in alcohol/drug publications.

The sources listed below are journals, newsletters, and indexes that review audiovisuals on a variety of alcohol and drug topics, including family issues. These publications provide bibliographic information--title, version or edition (if applicable), purchase/rental source, format(s), running time, cost, and year of release--and most have summaries and/or evaluations. Curricula and other educational literature, such as the literature guides and resource manuals by Robert Ackerman and Bryan Robinson (see items 1 and 107), can also be valuable guides to COA/ACOA films.

185

## Reviewing Sources

**Adolescent Counselor.** Bellevue, WA: A/D Communications Corp., 1988-- (bimonthly). Features a regular "Reviews" section which frequently includes audiovisual materials. Reviews consist of extensive summaries, recommendations, and complete bibliographic information.

**Alcoholism and Addiction.** Cleveland, OH: International Publishing Group, 1980-- (bimonthly). Includes an "Audio/Video Reviews" section that has been a regular department since 1987. Reviews provide evaluative recommendations and complete bibliographic information (except release date).

**Film and Video Finder.** Albuquerque, NM: National Information Center for Educational Media, 1987-- (irregular). This index, popularly known as NICEM, is available in print and as an online and CD-Rom database (known as "A-V Online"). Films and videos are listed under broad subject headings. Alcohol/drug material is usually included under the terms "guidance" or "psychology," but other related terms should also be checked. Entries contain a short description of content and complete bibliographic information.

**Prevention Forum.** Springfield, IL: Illinois Prevention Resource Center, 1980-- (quarterly). Film critiques were listed separately under a "Film Review" section until 1989; they are now included in the "Library Reviews" section. Complete bibliographic information and lengthy evaluations are provided.

**Prevention Pipeline.** Rockville, MD: Office for Substance Abuse Prevention, 1987-- (bimonthly). This current awareness publication is distributed by the National Clearinghouse for Alcohol and Drug Information. The "New Program Resources" section highlights both government and commercial videotapes on alcohol and other drug use.

Includes brief reviews and complete bibliographic information.

**Projection: An Audiovisual Review Service.** Toronto: Addiction Research Foundation, 1971-- (monthly). Includes evaluations of films and videocassettes reviewed by the Addiction Research Foundation Audio Visual Assessment Committee. Provides synopsis, scientific accuracy of material, general evaluation, recommended audience, complete bibliographic information, and subject headings. Offers periodic title and subject indexes.

**SALIS News.** Berkeley, CA: Substance Abuse Librarians and Information Specialists, 1981-- (quarterly). Includes brief film and video evaluations with subject, audience level, rating, and producer/distributor information.

**Student Assistance Journal.** Troy, MI: Performance Resource Press, 1988-- (five times per year). Features a "Media Resources" department with a section on films and tapes. Reviews include brief summaries and complete bibliographic information.

**Video Rating Guide for Libraries.** Santa Barbara, CA: ABC-CLIO, 1990-- (quarterly). New publication with lengthy video evaluations. Materials are critiqued by an outside panel of education and media specialists. Alcohol/drug videos are listed in the "Social Sciences" section under the subheading "Social Issues and Services." Reviews include one-to-five-star rating, complete bibliographic and cataloging information, and synopsis.

## Producers and Distributors

This selected list of audiovisual producers and distributors includes companies and organizations that supply only COA/ACOA films or those that offer a significant number of items about alcohol/drugs and family issues. Each of these organizations will supply a catalog on request. Company representatives can also be helpful in choosing a suitable film for special needs.

**Addiction Research Foundation**
Sales and Promotion Dept.
33 Russell St.
Toronto, Ontario
Canada M5S 2S1
(416) 595-6123

**AIMS Media**
6901 Woodley Ave.
Van Nuys, CA 91406
(800) 367-2467

**Children of Alcoholics Foundation, Inc.**
P.O. Box 4185
Grand Central Station
New York, NY 10163
(212) 351-2680

**Coronet/MTI Film and Video**
108 Wilmot Rd.
Deerfield, IL 60015
(800) 621-2131

**FMS Productions**
P.O. Box 4428
520 East Montecito St., Suite F
Santa Barbara, CA 93140
(800) 421-4609

**Gerald T. Rogers Productions, Inc.**
5215 Old Orchard Rd., Suite 990
Skokie, IL 60077
(800) 227-9100

**Guidance Associates**
Communications Park

Box 3000
Mount Kisco, NY 10549
(800) 431-1242


**Hazelden Educational Materials**
Pleasant Valley Rd.
Box 176
Center City, MN 55012
(800) 328-9000

**Human Services Institute**
P.O. Box 14610
Bradenton, FL 34280
(813) 746-7088

**Johnson Institute**
7151 Metro Blvd.
Minneapolis, MN 55435
(800) 231-5165

**Kinetic, Inc.**
255 Delaware Ave., Suite 340
Buffalo, NY 14202
(716) 856-7631

**MAC Publishing**
5005 East 39th Ave.
Denver, CO 80207
(303) 331-0148

**National AudioVisual Center**
8700 Edgeworth Dr.
Capitol Heights, MD 20743
(800) 638-1300

**Parker Productions**
30 West 39th Ave.
San Mateo, CA 94403
(800) 227-2463

**Pyramid Film and Video**
Box 1048
Santa Monica, CA 90406
(800) 421-2304

**Sunburst Communications**
101 Castleton St.
Pleasantville, NY 10570
(800) 431-1934

# APPENDIX C

## Periodicals

The following resources include journals, magazines, and newsletters that offer material on children and adult children of alcoholics as well as related family issues. Although many professional and research journals from a wide range of disciplines occasionally contain COA literature, this list covers only alcohol and drug periodicals that frequently include such items.

**A.A. Grapevine,** Alcoholics Anonymous, 468 Park Ave. South, New York, NY 10016. 1944-- (monthly). Shares personal experiences and feelings of Alcoholics Anonymous members regarding sobriety, recovery, and the Twelve Steps and Twelve Traditions.

**Addiction Letter,** Manisses Communications Group, P.O. Box 3357, Wayland Square, Providence, RI 02906-0357. 1985-- (monthly). Newsletter for professionals involved in treatment or prevention of alcohol and other drug problems. Highlights research, programs, materials, and events, including items dealing with COA and family issues. Annual index.

**Adolescent Counselor,** A/D Communications Corp., 8345 154th Ave. N.E., Redmond, VA 98052. 1988-- (bimonthly). Contains articles on intervention and treatment of substance abuse problems in adolescents. Includes regular columns on eating disorders, prevention and education, information for parents, upcoming events, and reviews of print and audiovisual materials. Occasional articles focus on children of alcoholics or related family issues.

**Advances in Alcohol and Substance Abuse,** Haworth Press, 10 Alice St., Binghamton, NY 13904-1580. 1981-- (quarterly). Covers research and clinical studies on substance abuse. Most issues have special themes--e.g., "Alcohol and Substance Abuse in Women and Children," and "Children of Alcoholics."

**Alateen Talk,** Al-Anon Family Groups, P.O. Box 862, Midtown Station, New York, NY 10018-0862. 1965-- (bimonthly). Official newsletter of the Alateen fellowship. Shares experiences of members and provides suggestions for meeting topics. Also useful for professionals working with children of alcoholics.

**Alcohol Health and Research World,** Superintendent of Documents, U.S. Government Printing Office, Washington, DC 20402. 1973-- (quarterly). Provides detailed descriptions of current research, treatment practices, and prevention programming. Covers all aspects of alcohol and its use, including children of alcoholics. Produced by the National Institute on Alcohol Abuse and Alcoholism for researchers, professionals, and interested laypersons. Annual index.

**Alcoholism: Clinical and Experimental Research,** Williams and Wilkins, 428 East Preston St., Baltimore, MD 21202-3993. 1977-- (bimonthly). Publishes research on biomedical and psychological aspects of alcohol use, alcoholism, and related problems. Includes articles on children of alcoholics, genetic markers, and familial transmission of alcoholism. Annual index.

**Alcoholism and Addiction,** International Publishing Group, 4959 Commerce Parkway, Cleveland, OH 44128. 1980--

(bimonthly). Offers feature articles and highlights of events of interest to practitioners, recovering alcoholics, and family members. Includes many articles for and about children and adult children of alcoholics and also contains book and audiovisual reviews. Formerly **Alcoholism/The National Magazine**.

**Alcoholism Treatment Quarterly**, Haworth Press, 10 Alice St., Binghamton, NY 13904-1580. 1984-- (quarterly). Designed for alcohol practitioners. Covers topics related to individual, group, and family therapy (including codependency).

**American Journal of Drug and Alcohol Abuse**, Marcel Dekker, 270 Madison Ave., New York, NY 10016. 1974-- (quarterly). Publishes research on medical, clinical, and social aspects related to the study and treatment of alcohol and drug abuse. Sponsored by the American Academy of Psychiatrists in Alcoholism and Addictions. Annual index.

**Brown University Digest of Addiction Theory and Application (DATA)**, Manisses Communications Group, P.O. Box 3357, Wayland Square, Providence, RI 02906-0357. 1981-- (eights times per year). Summarizes published research on alcoholism and other drug dependencies from scholarly journals around the world. Includes research on children of alcoholics and family risk factors. Annual index.

**Changes--For and About Adult Children**, U.S. Journal of Drug and Alcohol Dependence, Enterprise Center, 3201 S.W. 15th St., Deerfield Beach, FL 33442. 1986-- (bimonthly). Contains articles specifically on ACOA issues. Includes such topics as recovery, relationships, and family experiences. Features well-known therapists and famous personalities who are adult children of alcoholics.

**Contemporary Drug Problems**, Federal Legal Publications, 157 Chambers St., New York, NY 10007. 1971-- (quarterly). Focuses on social and legal aspects of alcohol and drug use. Covers codependency and dysfunctional families. Annual index.

**The Counselor,** National Association of Alcoholism and Drug Abuse Counselors (NAADC), 3717 Columbia Pike, Suite 300, Arlington, VA 22204. 1983-- (bimonthly). Offers special theme issues for counselors involved in addictions treatment. Topics include codependency, family therapy, and children at risk, as well as treatment approaches for substance abuse. Contains highlights of important events and also brief book and video reviews.

**Focus: Educating Professionals in Family Recovery,** U.S. Journal of Drug and Alcohol Dependence, Enterprise Center, 3201 S.W. 15th St., Deerfield Beach, FL 33442. 1978-- (bimonthly). Publishes feature articles and regular departments dealing with substance abuse and families. Covers treatment and recovery issues with frequent articles on children and adult children. Written for family members and therapists. Journal title has changed frequently: **Focus on Alcohol and Drug Issues, Focus on Family and Chemical Dependency,** and **Focus on Chemically Dependent Families.**

**The Forum,** Al-Anon Family Groups, P.O. Box 862, Midtown Station, New York, NY 10018-0862. 1953-- (monthly). Shares experiences of Al-Anon and Alateen members on coping with substance abuse in the family. Includes a calendar of special Al-Anon and Alateen events.

**Journal of Studies on Alcohol,** Rutgers Center of Alcohol Studies, P.O. Box 969, Piscataway, NJ 08855-0969. 1940-- (bimonthly). Publishes research on all aspects of alcohol use and alcohol-related problems. Includes research on family issues and family therapy as well as studies specific to children and adult children of alcoholics. Annual index.

**The NACoA Network,** National Association for Children of Alcoholics, 31582 Coast Highway, Suite B, South Laguna, CA 92677. 1985-- (quarterly). Official newsletter of NACoA.

Highlights upcoming conferences and other important events, activities of state chapters, and new resources for children of alcoholics and professionals who work with them.

**Perrin and Treggett's Review,** P.O. Box 561, Rocky Hill, NJ 08553. 1983-- (irregular). Newsletter of information for and about children of alcoholics, adult children, and therapists who deal with these populations. Includes brief listings of conferences and workshops. Formerly **COA Review.**

**Student Assistance Journal,** Performance Resource Press, 2145 Crooks Rd., Suite 103, Troy, MI 48084. 1988-- (five times per year). Offers feature articles, upcoming events, book and audiovisual reviews for educators and counselors working with student alcohol and drug problems. Focuses on identification and prevention of alcohol/drug problems, with occasional articles specifically on COA issues.

# AUTHOR INDEX

197

# TITLE INDEX

(*Note: In some cases, longer titles have been shortened.)

# SUBJECT INDEX

Abandonment, 94, 217, 219,
227, 233, 251, 259, 303,
311-13, 321, 341
Abstention, 193
Abstinence, 273
Acceptance, 29, 202, 217,
238, 308
Acetaldehyde: level of,
measurement, 14
Achenbach Child Behavior
Checklist, 21
Achievement, 189;
academic, 28, 101, 107
ACOA Quotient, 107
Acting-out: behavior, 116,
158; child, 61
Adaptation, 172
Addiction: stages of, 60,
151; warning signs of,
151
Addictions, multiple, 151
Addiction spiral, 249
Addictive disease concept,
151
Adjuster, 61
Adjustment: adult, 176;
behavioral, 12; in

children of alcoholics,
23; psychological, 107;
social, 24
Adolescence: as stage of
development, 251
Adoption studies, 10, 15,
18-19, 39, 129, 172
Adult children, male, 206
Adult Children of
Alcoholics Association,
342
Adult children of
alcoholics movement,
172
Adult Children of
Alcoholics Quotient,
107
Advertising, 96
Advocacy, 139
Affirmations, 82, 133, 205,
289-90, 321-22, 328,
333; developmental, 201
Aftercare, 71, 249
Age: effects of, on
children of alcoholics,
171, 284
Age regression, 331

## PUBLISHERS INDEX

The list below contains addresses for publishers and distributors of books and pamphlets cited in this sourcebook. To locate journal articles, consult your local public or academic library or use **APPENDIX C: Periodicals** to find addresses for many journals and magazines that frequently contain literature on children of alcoholics.

A.C.A.T. Press
1275 Fourth St.
Santa Rosa, CA 95404

Accelerated Development,
    Inc.
3400 Kilgore Ave.
Muncie, IN 47304

Al-Anon Family Group
    Headquarters, Inc.
P.O. Box 862
Midtown Station
New York, NY 10018-0862

Alcoholism Services of
    Cleveland
2490 Lee Blvd. #300
Cleveland Heights, OH
    44118

American College Health
    Association
1300 Piccard Dr.
Rockville, MD 20850

Aspen Publishers, Inc.
1600 Research Blvd.
Rockville, MD 20850

Babes World
17330 Northland Park Ct.
Southfield, MI 48075

Ballantine Books
Division of Random
    House, Inc.
400 Hahn Rd.
Westminster, MD 21157

Bantam Books
666 Fifth Ave.
New York, NY 10103

Bete, Channing L., Co.
South Deerfield, MA 01373

Bradbury Press
Distributed by Macmillan
	Publishing Co., Inc.
Front and Brown Sts.
Riverside, NJ 08370

Brae, Bonnie, Publications
12 Pickens Lane
Weaverville, NC 28787

Broadman Press
127 Ninth Ave. North
Nashville, TN 37234

Caron Institute
Box 277
Wernersville, PA 19565

CASPAR Alcohol Education
	Program
226 Highland Ave.
Somerville, MA 02143

Children of Alcoholics
	Foundation, Inc.
200 Park Ave.
31st Floor
New York, NY 10166

Chintillga Press
P.O. Box 6399
Dunedin, New Zealand

Choices Press
P.O. Box 2411
Monterey, CA 93942

Collier Books
Division of Macmillan
	Publishing Co., Inc.
Front and Brown Sts.
Riverside, NJ 08370

Community Intervention,
	Inc.
529 South Seventh St.
Suite 570
Minneapolis, MN 55415

CompCare Publishers
2415 Annapolis Lane
Minneapolis, MN 55441

Crown Publishers
225 Park Ave. South
New York, NY 10003

DePaul Rehabilitation
	Hospital
4143 South 13th St.
Milwaukee, WI 53221

Do It Now Foundation
P.O. Box 27568
Tempe, AZ 85285-7568

Dolphin/Doubleday
*See* Doubleday

Doubleday
Division of Bantam
    Doubleday Dell
    Publishing Group
666 Fifth Ave.
New York, NY 10103

Facts on File Publications
460 Park Ave. South
New York, NY 10016

Fireside/Learning
    Publication
Division of Simon and
    Schuster
1230 Avenue of the
    Americas
New York, NY 10020

Franklin, Charles, Press
7821-175th St. S.W.
Edmonds, WA 98020

The Free Press
Division of Macmillan
    Publishing Co., Inc.
Front and Brown Sts.
Riverside, NJ 08370

Gardner Press
19 Union Square West
New York, NY 10003

Genesis Publishing Co.
Box #228
Malvern, PA 19355
(distributed by Perrin and
    Treggett, Booksellers)

Glen Abbey Books
P.O. Box 19762
Seattle, WA 98109

Greenwillow Books
Division of William
    Morrow and Co.
105 Madison Ave.
New York, NY 10016

Greenwood Press
88 Post Road West
Westport, CT 06881

Guilford Press
72 Spring St.
New York, NY 10012

Gurze Books
P.O. Box 2238
Carlsbad, CA 92008

Harper and Row
10 East 53rd St.
New York, NY 10022

Haworth Press, Inc.
10 Alice St.
Binghamton, NY 13904-
    1580

Hazelden Educational
    Materials
Box 176
Pleasant Valley Rd.
Center City, MN 55012-
    0176

Health Communications,
   Inc.
Enterprise Center
3201 S.W. 15th St.
Deerfield Beach, FL 33442

Herald House/
   Independence Press
P.O. Box HH
3225 South Noland Rd.
Independence, MO 64055

Herald Press
616 Walnut Ave.
Scottdale, PA 15683

Houghton Mifflin
Wayside Rd.
Burlington, MA 01803

Human Sciences Press
Distributed by Independent
   Publishers Group
814 North Franklin
Chicago, IL 60610

Human Services Institute
P.O. Box 14610
Bradenton, FL 34280

Johnson Institute Books
7151 Metro Blvd.
Minneapolis, MN 55439-2122

Jossey-Bass Publishers
433 California St.
San Francisco, CA 94104

Knopf, Alfred A.
Subsidiary of Random
   House, Inc.
400 Hahn Rd.
Westminster, MD 21157

Learning Publications, Inc.
P.O. Box 1326
Holmes Beach, FL 34218

Lexington Books
Distributed by D.C. Heath
   and Co.
2700 Richardt Ave.
Indianapolis, IN 46219

Lifeline Press, Ltd.
3145 Geary Blvd.
Suite 520
San Francisco, CA 94118

MAC Publishing
5005 East 39th Ave.
Denver, CO 80207

Manisses Communications
P.O. Box 3357
Wayland Square
Providence, RI 02906-0357

Morrow, William, and Co.
105 Madison Ave.
New York, NY 10016

NAL Books
New American Library
120 Woodbine St.
Bergenfield, NJ 07621

National Association for
Children of Alcoholics
(NACoA)
31582 Coast Highway
Suite B
South Laguna, CA 92677

National Clearinghouse for
Alcohol and Drug
Information (NCADI)
P.O. Box 2345
Rockville, MD 20852

National Foundation for
Alcoholism
Communications
352 Halladay
Seattle, WA 98109

National Technical
Information Service
5285 Port Royal Rd.
Springfield, VA 22161

New York State Division of
Alcoholism and Alcohol
Abuse
194 Washington Ave.
Albany, NY 12210

Norton, W.W., and Co.
500 Fifth Ave.
New York, NY 10110

Nurturing Networks, Inc.
2820 West Main
Rapid City, MN 57702

Operation Cork
8939 Villa LaJolla Dr.
Suite 203
San Diego, CA 92037

PaperJacks Ltd.
330 Steelcase Rd. East
Markham, Ontario L3R
2M1
Canada

Parkside Medical Services
Corp.
205 West Touhy Ave.
Park Ridge, IL 60068

Performance Resource
Press
2145 Crooks Rd.
No. 103
Troy, MI 48084

Perrin and Treggett,
Booksellers
P.O. Box 190
Rutherford, NJ 07070

PICADA
2000 Fordem Ave.
Madison, WI 53704

Putnam's, G.P., Sons
200 Madison Ave.
New York, NY 10016

Quotidian
Box D
Delaware Water Gap, PA
   18327
(distributed by Perrin and
   Treggett, Booksellers)

Raintree Childrens Books
310 West Wisconsin Ave.
Mezzanine Level
Milwaukee, WI 53203

Recovery Publications
1201 Knoxville St.
San Diego, CA 92110

Research Institute on
   Alcoholism
1021 Main St.
Buffalo, NY 14203

Rhode Island Youth
   Guidance Center
*See* Manisses
   Communications

Rosen Publishing Group
29 East 21st St.
New York, NY 10010

Rutgers Center of Alcohol
   Studies
Publications Dept.
P.O. Box 969
Piscataway, NJ 08855-0969

St. Martin's Press
175 Fifth Ave.
New York, NY 10010

Scholastic Book Services
P.O. Box 75022931 East
McCarty St.
Jefferson City, MO 65102

Science and Behavior
Books
P.O. Box 60519
Palo Alto, CA 94306

Sitka Council on
   Alcoholism and Other
   Drug Abuse (SCAODA)
Community Education and
   Prevention
207 Moller
Sitka, AK 99835

STEM Publications
P.O. Box 8307
Tucson, AZ 85738

TAB Books
Blue Ridge Summit, PA
   17294-0850

Tarcher, Jeremy P.
Distributed by St. Martin's
   Press

U.S. Government Printing
   Office
Superintendent of
   Documents
Washington, DC 20402

Viking Penguin
40 West 23rd St.
New York, NY 10010

Warner Books
666 Fifth Ave.
New York, NY 10103

Watts, Franklin, Inc.
387 Park Ave. South
New York, NY 10016

Whitman, Albert, and Co.
5747 West Howard St.
Niles, IL 60648

Wiley, John, and Sons,
    Inc.
605 Third Ave.
New York, NY 10158-0012

Wisconsin Clearinghouse
P.O. Box 1468
Madison, WI 53701-1468

Youth and Shelter
    Services
232-1/2 Main St.
P.O. Box 1628
Ames, IA 50010